D1765784

# ÆSTHETICS

# Æsthetics
## LECTURES AND ESSAYS

---

## EDWARD BULLOUGH

### LATE PROFESSOR OF ITALIAN
### CAMBRIDGE UNIVERSITY

---

### EDITED WITH AN INTRODUCTION
### BY
## ELIZABETH M. WILKINSON

#### READER IN GERMAN IN THE
#### UNIVERSITY OF LONDON

## GREENWOOD PRESS, PUBLISHERS
### WESTPORT, CONNECTICUT

**Library of Congress Cataloging in Publication Data**

Bullough, Edward, 1880-1934.
    Aesthetics.

    Reprint of the 1957 ed. published by Stanford
University Press, Stanford, Calif.
        1.   Aesthetics--Addresses, essays, lectures.
I.   Title.
[BH221.G74B8  1977]                111.8'5          77-21814
ISBN 0-8371-9789-9

Originally published in 1977 by Stanford University Press

Reprinted with the permission of Stanford University Press

Reprinted in 1977 by Greenwood Press, Inc.

Library of Congress Catalog Card Number 77-21814

ISBN 0-8371-9789-9

Printed in the United States of America

# PREFACE

Edward Bullough spoke of æsthetics as his 'intellectual hobby'. This understatement was no doubt partly due to the modesty which characterised him. But it may very well be that in a mind as versatile as his that is what it really looked like seen from the inside. The fruits of this hobby, however, form the bulk of his published work, and nowhere do they bear the stamp of the dilettante, except in the most original sense of this word. His reputation as an æsthetician rests, it is true, on a single essay: ' "Psychical Distance" as a Factor in Art and an Æsthetic Principle.' But this essay has, as the author of a recent and important book on the philosophy of art puts it, become deservedly famous.[1] His contributions to experimental æsthetics, on the other hand, substantial though they were, have not, according to Sir Herbert Read, received the recognition they deserve, especially abroad.[2]

Less tangible, but not less important, evidence of the seriousness with which this hobby was pursued, is the influence he exerted on a generation of Cambridge students by the lectures he delivered annually from 1907 until shortly before his death—to the alarm of some senior members of the University, who looked askance at so strange a science, to the delight and edification of the undergraduates themselves. They, as I know from the testimony of many among my present colleagues, retain vivid and grateful memories of their rare combination of critical rigour and infectious enthusiasm.

I myself first heard his name from the late Susan Stebbing, whose own lectures on æsthetics were an unforgettable and formative experience, and, as she freely acknowledged, deeply indebted

---

[1] Susanne K. Langer, *Feeling and Form*, New York, 1953, p. 318.
[2] *Education through Art*, London, 1943, p. 90 f.

to his approach. The selection of his essays which appears in this volume reflects, I suppose inevitably, her opinion of what is most important and lasting in his published work. And but for her I should never have possessed one of the rare copies of his privately printed lectures.

Bullough produced no system of æsthetics, and these lectures certainly do not represent one. But they do something which systems of æsthetics and theories of art often omit to do or do only by implication: they start at the beginning and, just because they are introducing a new subject to the uninitiated, they set forth in an explicit and straightforward fashion exactly what æsthetics is. Perhaps even more important still, they tell us what it is not. It is the occupational risk of writers on any subject that they will almost certainly be grumbled at for not doing what they never set out to do. Writers on æsthetics, philosophy of art, art-history and art-criticism run the risk more than most, partly because of the ambiguities of the word *æsthetic* itself. If words can do anything at all to remove deep-seated misconceptions, Bullough's lucid words on the frontiers and interrelations of these cognate fields should do much.

Straightforward does not mean over-simplified or superficial. Bullough expended as much care on his lectures as on his work for publication. But it means, among other things, that style and tempo are adjusted to listeners and not readers. I have not attempted to deprive them of their discursive and personal character. For it is precisely here that they are different from, and have certain advantages over, a book: the point which does not immediately get across, or is objected to, is taken up again, clarified, the objections countered, and even where the answer still does not wholly satisfy, some of the cross-purposes have at least been uncrossed. My editorial activity has been confined to typography, punctuation, and the removal of phrases and passages which seemed redundant on the page.

The two essays in this volume are reprinted, without alteration except for the correction of misprints and the addition of an explanatory note, by kind permission of the Editor of *The British Journal of Psychology*. If the lectures define and plot the field of æsthetics, these essays make important contributions to some aspects of the field. The first, on 'Psychical Distance', elaborates an essential feature of all æsthetic experience, whether in art or in life, in appreciation or creation; whereas in the second, on 'Mind and Medium in Art', the distinction between creation and appreciation is sharply drawn. For it was Bullough's firm conviction that, closely related as they undoubtedly are, the one cannot be subordinated to the other without the risk of not doing justice to either. Again, he propounds here no theory of art, though it is clear enough to what kind of theory he inclines. But, together, these essays form a useful propædeutic to the study of any philosophy of art, by their uncovering of problems and clarification of concepts. The selection thus offers a coherence of material. Coherence of point of view is ensured by the integrity of Bullough's mind. For all his tolerance, he wrote from profound convictions and with unfailing consistency of direction.

I, unfortunately, never knew him. But I am indebted to many who have filled out for me the picture of the man: to his former pupils, Professor L. W. Forster and Professor C. P. Magill, for lending me their notes of his lectures on literature and criticism; to Professor L. A. Willoughby for lively reminiscences of common service in the secret world of Room 40 at the Admiralty—of Bullough's complete command of a difficult situation as chief interpreter of the Naval Armistice Commission, of his pedagogic versatility in holding the lower deck enthralled with an impromptu talk on German geography during the voyage to Kiel. This protagonist of æsthetics and æsthetic experience was clearly no æsthete. But my chief thanks are due to his widow and to his son, Father Sebastian Bullough, O.P., for having so readily placed at my disposal the biographical and bibliographical material I needed.

E.M.W.

*March 1954*

# CONTENTS

# BIOGRAPHICAL NOTE

Edward Bullough was born on 28 March 1880 at Thun in Switzerland of a Lancashire father and a German mother. After a Classical education at the Vitzthum Gymnasium in Dresden he went up to Trinity College, Cambridge, to read for the Medieval and Modern Languages Tripos. From 1902, when he graduated, he taught French, German, and Russian in the University, and in 1907 he also began to lecture on Æsthetics, the first course of its kind to be given in Cambridge. His interest in architecture brought him, in 1909, the arduous Secretaryship of the newly established Faculty Board of Architecture. In 1912 he was elected Fellow of Gonville and Caius College.

During the first world war Bullough served, as Lieutenant in the R.N.V.R., in the Intelligence Department at the Admiralty, and in 1918 went with the Naval Armistice Commission to Kiel. His reputation as a linguist also brought him the distinction, and the labour, of serving on the Government Committee appointed in 1916 to enquire into the position of Modern Languages in the Educational System of Great Britain, and he was intimately connected with the reform of the Modern Languages Tripos undertaken in the light of the Committee's recommendations.

The end of the war saw him active again as teacher and administrator. He became University Lecturer in German, Secretary to the Board of Fine Arts as well as to that of Modern Languages, Chairman of Council of the Modern Languages Association and Secretary of the Royal Commission on the Universities of Oxford and Cambridge. In 1923 he resigned his Lectureship in German to become University Lecturer in Italian. His love of that language went back to his boyhood; in 1908 he had married the daughter of Duse, and more and more he found that all his varied studies led him back to Italy as the fountain-head of European culture. This change coincided with his being received into the Church of Rome. In this sphere, too, he was active and distinguished. He became a Dominican Tertiary, member of the Universities Catholic Education Board and, in 1927, President of *Pax Romana*. Meanwhile in 1924 the Royal Institute of British Architects had recognised his services to architecture by making him an Honorary Associate, and in 1933 his academic career was crowned by his election to the Chair of Italian in Cambridge, barely a year before his untimely death on 17 September 1934.

For more detailed information the reader is referred to the Memoirs in

1. *The Caian* (the journal of Gonville and Caius College), Vol. XLIII, 1934. By M[ichael] O[akeshott].
2. *The Cambridge Review*, Vol. LVI, No. 1364, 1934. By E. K. Bennett.
3. *The Dublin Review*, Vol. 196, No. 392, 1935. By H. O. Evennett.

# PUBLICATIONS

## ÆSTHETICS

1. 1904. 'Matter and Form', *The Modern Language Quarterly* [London], VII, 1, pp. 10–15.
2. 1907. *The Modern Conception of Æsthetics*. A Course of Lectures delivered in the University of Cambridge. Privately printed, 105 pp.
3. 1907. 'On the Apparent Heaviness of Colours', *The British Journal of Psychology*, II, 2, pp. 111–52.
4. 1908. 'The "Perceptive Problem" in the Æsthetic Appreciation of Single Colours', ibid., II, 4, pp. 406–63.
5. 1910. 'The "Perceptive Problem" in the Æsthetic Appreciation of Simple Colour-Combinations', ibid., III, 4, pp. 406–47.
6. 1912. ' "Psychical Distance" as a Factor in Art and an Æsthetic Principle', ibid., V, 2, pp. 87–118. (Reprinted by M. Rader in *A Modern Book of Æsthetics*, New York, 1935, 2nd edition, 1952.)
7. 1913. *Ein Beitrag zur genetischen Ästhetik*. A Paper read at the first International Congress of Æsthetics in Berlin, 1913, 17 pp.
8. 1919. 'The Relation of Æsthetics to Psychology.' A Paper read before a General Meeting of the British Psychological Society on 31 May 1919. *The British Journal of Psychology*, X, 1, pp. 43–50.
9. 1920. 'Mind and Medium in Art.' A contribution to the Symposium presented at the Congress of Philosophy in Oxford, 24-7 September 1920, ibid., XI, 1, pp. 26–46.
10. 1921. 'Recent Work in Experimental Æsthetics', ibid., XII, 1, pp. 76–99.

## LITERARY AND CULTURAL STUDIES

11. 1905. 'Bibliographisches zu Schillers *Demetrius*', *Studien zur vergleichenden Literaturgeschichte*, 5, Ergänzungsheft, pp. 290–3.

12. 1916. (Together with A. P. Goudy.) An Edition, with Notes, of Tolstoy's *Sevastopol*, London, 1916.

13. 1920. *Cambridge Readings in Italian Literature*. An Anthology. Cambridge University Press, xviii, 335 pp.

14. 1920. 'The Civil Service and Modern Languages', *The Year Book of Modern Languages*, 1920, pp. 10–24.

15. 1921. 'The Relation of Literature to History', *Modern Languages*, II, pp. 37–47.

16. 1925. *Dante, the Poet of St. Thomas*. A Lecture delivered at the Summer School of Catholic Studies. *St. Thomas Aquinas*, Summer School Series, Heffer, Cambridge, pp. 247–84.

17. 1928. *Broken Bridges* (cultural, philosophical, etc.). Presidential Address at the International Conference of *Pax Romana* at Cambridge in 1928. *University Catholic Review*, II, 1, pp. 7–11.

18. 1932. *Dante und die Europäische Kultur*. Lecture delivered at the Salzburg Hochschulwoche, 1932.

19. 1932. *Dante als Vertreter des XIII. Jahrhunderts*. Lecture delivered at the Salzburg Hochschulwoche, 1932.

20. 1933. 'The Relation of Literature and the Arts', *Modern Languages*, XIV, pp. 101–12.

21. 1934. *Italian Perspectives*. An Inaugural Lecture. Cambridge University Press, 68 pp.

## TRANSLATIONS

22. 1924. *The Philosophy of St. Thomas Aquinas.* From the French of E. Gilson, Heffer, Cambridge; 2nd edition (incorporating elements included in the 3rd French edition of 1927), 1929, 287 pp.

23. 1930. *Two Essays* by Karl Adam (*Christ and the Western Mind; Love and Belief*), Sheed & Ward, London, 79 pp.

24. 1933. Revised translation from the Russian: *The Voyage of Captain Bellingshausen to the Antarctic Seas, 1819–21,* London, 1945.

25. 1934. *Essays in History,* by Pope Pius XI. Burns, Oates & Washbourne, London, 312 pp.

# INTRODUCTION

Good æstheticians may not be as few and far between as A. E. Housman alleged good critics to be. In rating these less common than returns of Halley's comet he displayed a perhaps too ardent perfectionism. But they are rare birds both, we must agree, æstheticians even rarer than critics. And for good reasons.

One of these is the nature of the subject-matter. The subject-matter of the critic does at least exist. There it is, plain for all to see, the picture, the statue, or the cathedral. And if the poem, the drama, and the music seem to lead a more elusive mode of existence, and to play a kind of ontological hide and seek, it is not with the critic that they play it, but with his more speculative brethren, the æsthetician and the philosopher. It will do him no harm to listen-in while they try their skill at a fashionable guessing-game: Where is the poem? On the page? In the mind? In whose mind? (childishly easy to parody, but indispensable questions for all that). It may even do him good, provided always that he can so assimilate their arguments and their answers that they affect his work in an indirect and unobtrusive way. But he can get on very well without bothering his head over such subtleties; not because his activity is less subtle than theirs, but because it begins where theirs leaves off. What matters for him, what he cannot begin to be subtle without, is an unassailable conviction that the work before him has a distinctive and meaningful reality of its own. Whether this conviction remains naïve or becomes philosophically enlightened is, to judge from the history of criticism, a matter of very little moment.

The subject-matter of the æsthetician is a much more dubious affair. The trouble is not that the study called æsthetics is a parvenu in the society of learning, and has not had time to find its feet.

Equally late-comers are already established, have their house set in order and are busy cultivating their garden. It is rather that what it sets out to study has not managed to get itself generally accepted, but is regarded, increasingly today and in surprisingly varied quarters, as something of an upstart too. Interest in Art with a capital A only emerged clearly in the eighteenth century, along with the modern system of the arts, fine arts as distinct from crafts.[1] This is not, of course, to say that art created before then was nothing but craft, or that there is no way of distinguishing art from craft (or that we ought not to try), or that there is no such thing as Art, but only an indefinite, and increasing, number of arts which no artificial concept, belatedly imposed, can ever make into a unity. But these things are said. And we find, for example, existentialist philosophers, among others, so busy 'rescuing' poetry back from Art to Language that they never bother to tell us how poetry differs from philosophy. In fact they seem to think there is no need. The two were one to begin with, their argument seems to go, and the sooner they become indistinguishable again the better. It is the same with appreciation. Interest in a distinctively æsthetic awareness only emerged in the eighteenth century too. Again this is not to say that the awareness itself was not there before. But some historians do say it. And that is enough for marxists, existentialists, and others who are vaguely anxious to 'save' art for Life, to regard this distinctive awareness as so much of an interloper into human nature, or Being, that they think to

---

[1] Cf. P. O. Kristeller, 'The Modern System of the Arts: A Study in the History of Æsthetics', *Journal of the History of Ideas*, 1951, vol. 12, pp. 496–527; 1952, vol. 13, pp. 17–46. Semantic evidence of the extreme gradualness of the emergence of Art and the Artist as distinct concepts is the fact that Schiller can still use Künstler (artist) of a watchmaker as late as 1795, and this in a treatise the express aim of which was to define the nature and function of Art in its modern sense (*On the Æsthetic Education of Man*, Letter III). The translation in the Bohn Library obscures the point by rendering Künstler here as 'mechanic'. So does the new one by Reginald Snell (London, 1954). Not so that by J. Weiss (London, 1849), though in other respects this is as unreliable and inadequate as the Bohn.

dispose of it by refusing to recognise its existence. What was not in the beginning (a beginning variously located as to time and place) is not now. Either it is 'really' something else, 'nothing but' the primitive needs and appetites to which it can be traced back; or else it is not 'grounded in original Being' and hence not existentially real at all.

Such confusion of origin with present significance is not to be lightly dismissed as a mere logical flaw, a typical instance of the genetic fallacy. Its roots go deeper than logic. They draw their sustenance from primitivistic tendencies in our age. The civilised, the sophisticated, the differentiated is complex, and complexity is too heavy a burden to bear. Let us therefore retreat from it into undifferentiated oneness or into the simplicity of primitive impulse. The attitude of certain linguistic philosophers, who put the æsthetic out of bounds for philosophical enquiry by relegating its symbols to the irrational, looks more like rejection than denial. But is it not, in its vain striving for unambiguous communication, yet another abdication from complexity, a rationally disguised covering action in the same retreat?

To these doubts and slurs cast upon the existence of the phenomena to be studied must be added the uncertainties introduced into the subject by the word chosen to designate them. It was, ironically enough, the 'Father of Æsthetics' himself, Baumgarten, who gave his progeny, *æsthetic* and its derivatives, such a bad start. What he originally aimed at with his *Æsthetica* (1750-8) was a logic of the imagination, a science of the 'dark ideas' known by the senses, to supplement logic, the science of the 'clear and distinct ideas' known by the mind. But by limiting the field to art, and by making his new science so narrowly normative, what he succeeded in evolving was a theory of art, and a criticism of taste, based on conventional criteria and traditional rules. Kant, in his *Critique of Pure Reason* (1781), protested against this misuse of the word and applied it, in accordance with its etymology ('αἴσθησις, perception by the senses, especially by feeling, but also by seeing, hearing, etc.'), to the 'science which treats of the conditions of sensuous perception'.[1] But Baumgarten's 'misapplication' established itself, and both meanings have persisted, in Germany and elsewhere, to be a source of continuing confusion.

Yet a third meaning, known and used in England at least since Pater, but not exhibited in the citations in the *New English Dictionary*, is that given to the word by Schiller in his *Letters on the Æsthetic Education of Man* (1795). Schiller obviously felt that in view of the prevailing ambiguity he could not be explicit enough; for although his treatise is itself an extended definition of æsthetic consciousness, an account of its genesis, mode of operation and function, he appended to his 20th *Letter* a long explanatory footnote[2] 'for the benefit of readers unfamiliar with the true meaning of this word so misused by the ignorant'. This meaning is at once narrower and wider than the others. It is narrower, because it refers not to perception in general but to one distinctive mode of it in particular. It is wider, because the field of operation is not confined to art; this mode of perception can assert itself in response to anything whatsoever; art is a special case within the general field, a highly significant case, because it is peculiarly designed to call forth this response. And this meaning is wider, too, because æsthetic perception in Schiller's sense involves the whole personality. Sense-activity it certainly is, but its distinctiveness does not lie there. It lies rather in a brief harmony of all the functions, feeling and thinking too. Subjectively, he further defines it as a state of precarious but infinitely fruitful equipoise; objectively, as the way things dispose themselves when they are contemplated for their own sake, without reference to purposes, ends, or causes. For Schiller, as for Schopenhauer, who developed these thoughts in famous and resounding passages of *The World as*

---

[1] A history of æsthetics would obviously have to deal with Kant's change of front in his *Critique of Judgment*, but I am here only concerned with the origins of the several meanings of the word.

[2] Omitted from the English translation in the Bohn Library, but to be found in those by J. Weiss (ed. cit., p. 129) and R. Snell (ed. cit., p. 99).

*Will and Idea*, the æsthetic is one way among others of being related to things. It takes its place alongside the physical (in which Schiller includes the life-serving, the practical), the logical (which also covers what we should call the scientific) and the ethical.[1] And what results from such æsthetic encounter is knowledge, not mere pleasurable sensation, intuitive knowledge, at once richly detailed and intensely clear, of the object in its concrete uniqueness.

What a falling off in the meaning of the word as we usually meet it in criticism today! How puny and spindly-legged it has become, its emaciation attested by the disparaging 'merely' which almost invariably precedes it! There are good historical reasons for this. One is that some of those who used the word in its fullest sense claimed more for the æsthetic mode than it can by its nature perform. Reaction was inevitable; and whatever guise it took, moralistic, socialistic, or Gilbertian, the form of attack was in one respect the same: instead of assigning the æsthetic attitude its proper limits, its opponents whittled away at the attitude itself, reducing it, from an encounter of the total personality with the totality of the work of art, to the pleasure, part sensory, part intellectual, afforded by the perception of formal relations abstracted from what they considered to be the really important thing about the work, namely its meaning or content. And rightly considered. The flaw was only in mistaking the nature of the content, in thinking that it is what is left when this abstraction of the 'æsthetic' aspect has been made, in not realising that it is implicit in the form itself. A familiar counter-reaction in favour of æsthetic values has only aggravated the situation. Anxious to dispel the misconception that what matters is content in this wrong sense, these advocates of 'pure form' go to all lengths to deny that

---

[1] Wyld's *Universal English Dictionary* approximates to Schiller's meaning with the example: '*æsthetic point of view, criticism* (contrasted with *scientific* or *historical*)', but confuses the issue by making it synonymous with *criticism*.

æsthetic effect has anything whatsoever to do with content;[1] or else they insist that in a work of art form *is* content, that they are not only inseparable but are one and the same thing. The æsthetic effect in its purity is, according to them, confined to a specific 'æsthetic emotion', which has nothing to do with ordinary feeling, but is akin to, if not identical with, the satisfaction felt by a mathematician on perceiving the rightness of the relations in the elegant solution of a problem. In art it is the delight attendant on the perception of such surface qualities as texture, sound, rhythm, proportions, grouping, etc. Artists themselves, when they become articulate about their work, often lend unwitting support to this view, partly because they are, in fact, extensively preoccupied with these very things, and partly because it is the aspect of the creative process most accessible to their conscious inspection. But the man in the street has a healthy instinct to disagree, to insist that there must be more to art than such highfalutin falderals. The critic in the journals, who at least pretends to be doing more than follow his instinct, helps him not at all to clarify this basically sound hunch, if he brushes aside the 'merely' æsthetic aspect of a work and exhorts him to respond to it *also* as moral protest, social document, or religious revelation (the operative word here is *also*). He may think he is countering the formal abstractions of the

---

[1] Such theorists and critics are always bewildered by Goethe's clear insistence that it is the content (*Gehalt*) of a work of art that ultimately matters. They cannot reconcile it with his no less clear insistence that the form is all-important, and assume that here must be one of his self-contradictions. This is not so. It can be freely admitted that Goethe was no stickler for either terminology or logic. But he was not a confused thinker, and above all not about poetry. It is significant that he never says that it is the *Stoff* (theme, subject-matter) or the *Inhalt* (a word used indiscriminately for contents, whether of a novel or a play, a jar or a box) of art that matters. *Gehalt* is rather that which inheres in, is implicit in the form: its import. This, he says, proceeds from the inner life of the artist. Cf. E. M. Wilkinson, *Goethe's Conception of Form. Annual Lecture on a Master Mind.* Henriette Hertz Trust of the British Academy, 1951. The only entirely satisfactory discussion of the form-content problem that I know is by Susanne Langer in *Feeling and Form*, ed. cit., p. 51 f.

æsthete. In reality he is subscribing to them, fostering the fragmentation of both the work and him who regards it, and further confounding the existing semantic confusion. And it is worse confounded still from the scientific side by the tendency of psychologists to hark back in their investigations to the supposed literal meaning of *æsthetic*, and test likes and dislikes, pleasure and displeasure. As was observed long ago,[1] if that is what æsthetics is concerned with, *apolaustic* would have been a more appropriate designation.

These, then, are some of the difficulties arising from the subjectmatter of æsthetics: the field is frayed and untidy at the edges, the ground in the middle inclined to give under the feet of anyone not possessed of the most lucid intelligence and the firmest convictions.

Another important reason for the scarcity of good æstheticians is the unlikelihood of all the required qualities and capacities coming together in one and the same human being. Without 'des principes fermement arrêtés et une passion très ardente', it has been said, there can be no serious criticism. And without this rare marriage there can be no serious æsthetics either. But the ideal union here is more complex still. Firm as his principles must be, the critic çan, and often does, arrive at them intuitively. His is an essentially practical activity; and unless it is a question of passing on his craft to others he does not need, and may not wish, to turn a critical eye on his own premises and procedures and articulate them in a logical way. The task of the æsthetician, by contrast, is essentially theoretical; and unless he is able and willing to examine the instruments of his thinking, weigh the merits and demerits of hypothesis and analogy, of induction and deduction, he had better not embark on it. This is the indispensable requirement. Yet, though he possess it, without sensitive and passionate experiences of art in its most varied manifestations, he will produce an æsthetic with firm bones but no flesh. And without wide knowledge of

---

[1] By Sir William Hamilton in a discussion of Baumgarten (*Lectures on Metaphysics and Logic*, 1859, I, vii, p. 124). Cited in the *New English Dictionary* under *æsthetic*.

experiences other than his own he will tend to force the facts to suit his theory. Ideally, he must be as discriminating *vis-à-vis* the concrete particulars of art as the critic, as observant of his own responses, and as tolerant of those of others, as the psychologist; but he needs, too, the philosopher's sensibility for discriminating abstractions and his power of appropriate generalisation. Last, but far from least, the history of the subject shows that unless his extra-æsthetic values are finely differentiated and firmly held he will either (as was more likely in the securer world of the nineteenth century) put an unwarranted trust in the power of art, through buoyant disregard of the shadow inevitably cast by things of great potency; or else (as is all too likely in the Angst-ridden world of today) deny its legitimate power through fear of its freedom, a freedom which the timorous heart may well mistake for caprice since its laws are immanent and not formulable as precepts.

Edward Bullough was one of the rare possessors of this many-sided equipment. And his interests were as varied as his talents. An accident of birth made him the immediate heir of more than one culture, and it was very likely an accident of education which gave him the firmest basis for any endeavour, namely the Classics. But the doubling of his modern languages from three to six—to English, French and German he added Russian, Spanish and Italian—was all his own merit. Nor did he rest content with the European tradition. His love of painting and architecture led him to devote two years to learning Chinese, in order, as he says, to have some direct contact with that civilisation. For his interest never stopped at the linguistic, or even at the literary. Its limit was nothing short of what he called the 'perspectives' of a civilisation. He could explore with singular historical subtlety the vastly different vistas opened up in the minds of an Englishman, a Frenchman, or a German by the same word of common speech, or catch from the casual remark of an Italian tram-driver the precise temper of his regard for the ancient culture lying all about him in his daily life, the exact blend of pride and easy familiarity, 'as towards a family possession'. To the pursuit of these perspectives, the discernment of the cultural backcloth of a people, he brought the same openness and sensibility as to works of art and literature, and it saved him from the anachronistic crudities, the local and historical parochialism, which are a blemish on much criticism and æsthetics. Yet all this together was but one side of his mind. He led, he says in his Inaugural Lecture, a sort of double life: this in the arts, and another in the sciences. He was welcomed into the distinguished circle of the founder-members of the British Psychological Society, counted among his friends neurologists such as Sir Henry Head and anthropologists such as W. H. R. Rivers. Here, too, his thoroughness was undaunted: he carried out experiments in the Cambridge Psychological Laboratories, attended classes held by the Director at the Fullbourn Asylum, sat at the feet of Sir Hugh Anderson to learn the physiology of the central nervous system, and even prepared sections of the spinal chord under his direction.

For the modern conception of æsthetics there could scarcely have been a more adequate preparation. And what subject could have offered the same scope for abilities so diverse and disparate? But if the subject as such gave them scope, it was what he himself made of the subject that integrated them. In an area so ill-defined and amorphous these several abilities might still have gone their unrelated ways, pulled in divergent directions and ended in ultimate dissipation. What harnessed them in mutual support was the predominantly organising temper of his mind: his fine sense for appropriate unities which can be abstracted from the diversity of phenomena and experiences, his firm grip on what makes each of these unities distinctive; his patient endeavour, first to co-ordinate them one with another, and then to subordinate them to a more all-embracing principle, that is, to generalise without obliterating differences. In this way he is able to do justice to the variety of art-forms resulting from accidents of history, climate, habitat, economic conditions, inventions, cultures, and yet at the same time insist that Art is unquestionably One; or to the variety of tastes conditioned by similar factors, and yet protest against anarchy in criticism, against individual caprice and arbitrary standards. Only in this way could he ever have arrived at a principle such as 'psychical distance', which allows for maximum diversity within a formula of elegant simplicity; or at his concept of 'æsthetic consciousness', which is wide enough to embrace appreciation and creation (and more) without falsifying either. The way he arrives at his goal is always as important as the goal itself. It would be idle to pretend that he raises all the problems. Still less that he gives all the answers. And if the reader is provoked to disagree with those he gives, so much the better—so long as he takes the trouble to refute them or tries to find better ones for himself. If he does either or both of these things with anything like Bullough's care for distinctions, he will have learned a great deal about æsthetic thinking, and indeed about thinking in general.

*     *     *

Bullough was an ardent protagonist of the psychological approach to æsthetics. His *Lectures* breathe the fresh optimism which the new science of psychology brought into this as into other fields at the turn of the century. Between 1905 and 1908 he himself carried out an extensive series of tests on the appreciation of colours, on the basis of which he made a classification of fundamental perceptive types. These experiments are described, and his own types correlated with those of Binet and others, in four articles on experimental æsthetics published in the *British Journal of Psychology*.[1] Sir Herbert Read in *Education Through Art*[2] points to further interesting parallels with Jung's four psychic functions and with the types he himself evolved on the basis of his researches into children's art.

[1] For details see the list of Bullough's publications, *supra*, p. xiii. In the following notes the articles are referred to by their number in that list.

[2] Ed. cit., p. 94. Cf. pp. 143–8 for his correlation of Bullough's types with his own based on investigations of children's art.

In his experiments Bullough relied entirely on introspective evidence. He was fully alive to the drawbacks and defects of this method, to the element of self-deception which must to some extent vitiate its conclusions. But he was convinced that there is, nevertheless, 'no other method for æsthetic experiments, the statistical method . . . serving no purpose whatever'.[1] For what he wanted to get at was not just the subjects' *opinion* of the colours but the *reasons* which prompted their judgment. 'I wanted to know . . . what was happening in their minds in reference to each particular colour.'[2] Of the statistical method he offers a critique.[3] Its first and chief fallacy is its distrust of introspective evidence as 'unscientific' because it is subjective. This is to mistake the kind of fact to be studied. The æsthetic 'fact' is a distinctive mode of *consciousness*. To study this on the lines of stimulus and response is to introduce a method wholly inappropriate to the material in hand. Bullough held this pseudo-scientific attitude responsible for the disrepute into which æsthetic experiments have deservedly fallen in the eyes of layman and scientist alike. Its second fallacy is its unjustified assumption that everything can be accounted for by one single principle. The mere numerical accumulation of facts affords no proof of the existence of any underlying principle unless it can be demonstrated, or at least reasonably assumed, that all the facts are due to the working of one and the same principle. But in æsthetic preferences there is nothing to indicate that one single reason is everywhere active. On the contrary, everything goes to show that they are prompted by a variety of reasons. Its third fallacy is the hedonistic conception of art underlying it. To rely on preference-judgments, as it must, is to ignore the crucial fact that,

---

[1] *Publications*, No. 3, p. 122.

[2] Ibid., No. 4, p. 412. L. A. Reid (*A Study in Æsthetics*, London, 1931, p. 56, fn. 2) in an account of Bullough's types draws attention to further snares of such experiments. Bullough would no doubt have replied, as he did to his own misgivings and reservations, that 'it is a case of making a virtue out of necessity'.

[3] *Publications*, No. 3, p. 127 f. and No. 4, pp. 411 ff., 459 ff.

in point of beauty, things are fundamentally *in*comparable. And it is to ignore the difference between the agreeable and the beautiful. For preference-judgments can only test quantity not quality. The mark of a beautiful thing, however, is not that it gives us more pleasure than an agreeable one—it may conceivably give less—but that it affects us in an entirely different way.

But whatever method they employ—about this Bullough was explicit and emphatic—experiments are never an end, but always only a means, a means to the comprehension of more complex and intricate æsthetic experiences.[1] All they can do is to test the 'elements' of such experiences by providing relatively simple conditions. And even then it must be realised that these elements will undergo some qualitative change when isolated in the artificial and forced conditions of experiment. The onus of interpretation is at no stage lifted from the experimenter. His aim can never be the reduction of the complex to the simple. It must always be the interpretation of the simple in the light of the complex and of the complex in the light of the simple.

These limitations granted and understood, experimentation has its uses. Of this Bullough was convinced, as he was and remained convinced that the future of æsthetics lay in psychology. At the end of his last published work on the subject he gives his considered reasons for this and assigns modern æsthetics its proper tasks. Since questions such as: What is beauty? What causes beauty? have proved insoluble, the only remaining line of attack is the problem of its effect.

> Until the conceptions with which Philosophies of Art are wont to operate are illuminated by actually and accurately observed experiences of many persons, instead of being vaguely apprehended and rashly generalised personal introspections of their authors, little good will be done by interminable discussions. . . . It is the concern of æsthetic theory and experiment to define and analyse æsthetic consciousness, to ascertain the conditions of its realisation

[1] Ibid., No. 3, p. 128 f.

and the range and typical features of its occurrence. If this attempt proves successful, theory will have attained to a fundamental generalisation in Æsthetics. For this consciousness, as a mental state *sui generis*, is the level of psychic life which must be reached and maintained, if æsthetic appreciation is to be realised. Appreciation will then not be dependent upon the presence of this or that mental process, upon pleasure or emotion, upon empathy or imagery or organic sensations. No; any mental state, from the obscurest organic feeling to the most abstract intellectual operation, may form the object of æsthetic appreciation—*provided it occurs within and on the level of the sphere of æsthetic consciousness.*[1]

That was in 1921. In 1953 the author of the most coherent and satisfying theory of art to appear in this century seems to turn the tables completely. 'The psychological approach', she writes, '. . . has not brought us within range of any genuine problems of art. So . . . we might do better to look upon the art object as something in its own right, with properties independent of our prepared reactions, properties which command our reactions. . . .'[2] Mrs. Langer has some hard things to say about psychological æsthetics; rightly, for it has failed miserably to live up to its promise. And by starting at the other end, with art itself instead of with its effects, she has found an answer to the crucial question which æstheticians have usually skirted, or else shirked altogether: What is it that art actually *creates*? Her answer is: Quite literally, an illusion, an illusion which in its turn serves the creation of forms symbolic of human feeling. Taking up Schiller's notion of semblance (*Schein*), she has worked out with philosophical precision the exact nature of the illusion created by each of the arts, and has thus achieved what Bullough thought could not reasonably be hoped for: she has found in the objective world of art 'a common feature of sufficient concreteness to make it applicable

---

[1] Ibid., No. 10, p. 99.
[2] Susanne K. Langer, *Feeling and Form*, ed. cit., p. 39. This return to the object reflects a parallel movement in the criticism of the last thirty years: in reaction against critical relativism a tendency to concentrate on structural analysis.

both to all works and to each one separately'.[1] Does this mean that his approach is now outdated? According to him, modern æsthetics has not to think primarily about the picture, but about our experience of the picture. According to her, its mistake has been to do just that. Are they completely at odds?

Not as much as might appear at first sight. He may champion psychology, but he is as suspicious of psychologism as she is; for they both know the vanity of trying to interpret all human interests as though they were oblique manifestations of animal needs. What he has in mind when he calls æsthetics a science is not the importation of inappropriate hypotheses from the natural sciences, but—to borrow a formulation from her[2]—'the great ideals of empiricism, namely observation, analysis and verification'; while her recoil from the psychological approach does not, of course, imply a return to speculative æsthetics cut loose from observation and experience. On the contrary. In requiring philosophy of art to 'begin in the studio, not in the gallery, auditorium or library',[3] she is prepared to exchange one kind of empirical evidence for another. Again her return to the art object is not to the old pursuit of criteria of beauty which are objective in the sense of being metrically demonstrable; while if he starts with the effect, it is not because he thinks everything can be reduced to effect, that works of art have no independent properties and principles of their own. Indeed, though they start off from opposite ends, at one important point they are in striking and almost verbal agreement. 'The question of what gives one the [æsthetic] emotion', says Professor Langer, 'is exactly the question of what makes the object artistic. . . .'[4] 'Its power to *compel* æsthetic adaptation', wrote Bullough, '. . . is, of course, what makes an object into a work of Art . . .'[5]

[1] *Lectures, infra*, p. 57.
[2] Op. cit., p. 35.
[3] Ibid., p. ix.
[4] Ibid., p. 34.
[5] *Publications*, No. 10, p. 98.

Yet it is on this very point that the real difference between them hinges. Her repudiation of psychological æsthetics is sustained by her settled conviction that art commands an appropriate response regardless of the attitude we bring with us when we come into its presence. How else explain why the world recognises works of art as public treasures? If æsthetic experience is such a sophisticated, rare, and artificial attitude as some of its modern apologists make out, then the fact 'that primitive peoples, from the cave-dwellers of Altamira to the early Greeks, should quite unmistakably have known what was beautiful, becomes a sheer absurdity'.[1]

Bullough was sceptical of this kind of reasoning. In a discerning little essay on 'The Relation of Æsthetics to Psychology' he points out that the greater part of what we call art was *not* art to the men who made it, and that it is an unwarranted substitution of our view of things to imagine that the men of Altamira or of Greece, or even of times nearer our own, experienced before art what we experience.[2] And if there is one thing that psychological æsthetics *has* been able to show us, it is that art may be cherished and esteemed for reasons quite other than æsthetic.

And he was altogether less sanguine about the power of art to compel an appropriate response. Not because he thought that æsthetic experience, as we know it today, is artificial, esoteric, or the property of the few. But he did think that it is a distinctive mode of awareness, gradually developed as an 'originally un-differentiated system of sentiments and conceptions became split into those separate strands of feeling, those distinct systems of ideas, which we have come to term Religion, Magic, Justice, Right, Truth, Craftsmanship, Art'[3]—a form of understanding which is natural to man, certainly, but second nature, given only potentially, actually realised by learning, and by choice. For differentiation has resulted in our having at our disposal several

[1] Op. cit., p. 38.
[2] *Publications*, No. 8, pp. 47 ff. Cf. his distinction between genetic and psychological æsthetics, 'Mind and Medium', *infra*, p. 152 f.
[3] *Publications*, No. 8, p. 48.

possible ways of responding to one and the same object, and people vary enormously in their ability to keep them distinct and in their power to switch flexibly from one to another. These personal variants prevail even in the face of objects, such as art objects, which are clearly designed to call forth one specific kind of response. Granted, the beauty of art is not in the eye of the beholder. Nevertheless in the perception of its beauty by any individual two sets of factors are always involved: those in the work and those in the percipient. However compelling the former, there are always those who fail to be compelled; just as there are always those in whom æsthetic adaptation is such a natural and habitual mode that they make this kind of response to objects not designed to evoke it. Bullough's position is summed up in the statement: 'Despite their intentional appeal, the conditions in which [works of art] produce their effects are variable and diverse.'[1]

This still holds good even if we can point to a property of art which survives logical analysis as triumphantly as illusion seems to do. The artist may declare he has created it. The philosopher can prove it exists, independent of our reactions. Once it enters into relation with us, however, it is always a question not only of something meant to illude but of someone to be illuded. And for those who don't respond at the æsthetic level it simply isn't 'there' or, as the tortuous history of the illusion theory makes abundantly and often amusingly clear, the wrong kind of illusion is there. Æsthetic illusion is only demonstrable to those who share experience of the æsthetic. And Mrs. Langer concedes as much when she says that 'in the work of a master hand the expressive form is so commanding ... that no one *who has discovered the phenomenon of artistic import at all* is likely to miss it there'.[2] (The italics are mine.) The reason so many do miss it today, she goes on, is because sensitivity to form is blunted by the jumble of styles sur-

---

[1] Ibid., p. 44. Cf. *Publications*, No. 10, p. 93 f. and p. 97 f.
[2] Op. cit., p. 53.

rounding us in our eclectic culture, by the tangle of historical lines all ending in the snarl we call civilisation. And yet—which seems rather contrary—she is impatient of the 'prepared' reaction, of the cultivation of an æsthetic attitude. 'It is part of the artist's business to make his work elicit this attitude instead of requiring the percipient to bring an ideal frame of mind with him.'[1]

To this Bullough would reply: Why make them alternatives? That indeed is the artist's business. It is our business to meet him half-way—not for his sake but for our own. And for the sake of our civilisation. (We can't unload all responsibility for it on to the artist any more than we can on to the scientist.) He would entirely agree with her that the most potent agency in art education is the body of art handed down to us and the art, or the pseudo-art, all around us. But he saw no reason why this 'silent, collective and largely anonymous pressure' should not be helped along, or corrected, by taking thought. In æsthetic perception, as in any other kind of perception, the nature of our predisposition matters enormously; whether it is voluntary or spontaneous very little.[2] Bullough was all for trying to raise our covert assumptions and preconceptions to the light of day. He was even heretical enough to dissent from the view that theory is the enemy of practice, and to believe that knowing something about æsthetics might favourably affect the expectancies we bring to art. Indeed in speaking of 'spontaneous modifications of taste through knowledge and reflexion'[3] he implies that the antinomy between 'prepared' and 'unprepared' is not as real as we might think.

Either way, the admission that what we bring with us affects what we see makes the case for psychological æsthetics. For if art is the essential factor in human life and culture that both those writers believe it to be, then it is as essential for the educator to

---

[1] Ibid., p. 318.

[2] As it seems to matter little to the result whether an artist creates spontaneously or with reflection.

[3] *Lectures, infra*, p. 18. Cf. his suspicions of 'purity in heart' in matters æsthetic, 'Mind and Medium', *infra*, p. 151.

know how people are, and how they do in fact respond, as to know what art is and what it is its function to effect. The latter is the business of art theory. The former part of the business of æsthetics. The two are not synonymous, though they are perpetually confused; and this latest book shows what need there still is for the kind of clarification which Bullough attempted. Art theory must indeed begin with art objects, and end, as Mrs. Langer's does, with their relation to the public. But this does not make psychological æsthetics redundant.[1] There is still need to explore the situations which then arise, to investigate the conditions of æsthetic adaptation, the varying facility of individuals to achieve it, or to maintain it for any length of time, how far disturbing factors can be either voluntarily overcome or are spontaneously set aside.[2] If modern æsthetics has gone wrong, it is not, Bullough was convinced, by starting at the wrong end—though he agreed that exaggerated enthusiasm for psychological methods had led to undue preoccupation with æsthetic effect[3]—but by losing sight of the fact that its concern is with a distinctive quality of experience: 'by studying emotion, pleasure, perception in general, instead of *æsthetic* perception, *æsthetic* pleasure, *æsthetic* emotion, by proceeding on exclusively subjective lines and failing to preserve continual contact with the objective world of art products.'[4] Without contact with these stable and most accessible concretions of æsthetic consciousness, it cannot hope to frame adequate generalisations.

His own principle of psychical distance certainly does not err in this respect; which no doubt explains why it has been built into the structure of the subject itself, and been a stimulus to workers in cognate fields—most excitingly, perhaps, to Jane Harrison who in her account of the birth of Greek tragedy out of religious rite

[1] Any more than the science of language precludes a science of how we use and interpret language.
[2] *Publications*, No. 10, p. 97 f.
[3] *Lectures, infra*, p. 63.
[4] Ibid., p. 62.

uses it to explain the difference of attitude between the participants in ritual and the spectators of drama.[1] The notion of distance has a long and distinguished ancestry. But at the end of the eighteenth century it took a new turn. Of Bullough's affiliations with German thought of that time, especially with Goethe and Schiller, I have written elsewhere.[2] From Schiller, in particular, he must have got the idea of shifting the notion of *éloignement* from poetics to æsthetics, from the physical to the psychical plane. For it was he who transformed it from a rule for poets (to distance their theme either in space or time) into a psychological statement about the quality of remoteness which all objects assume in the æsthetic relation.[3] And it was he who seems to have coined the verb, at any rate in this psychical sense, when he enjoined upon the poet to write, not in the grip of immediate emotion, but 'in the tranquillity of *distancing* recollection'.[4] As Bullough has elaborated it, the principle perfectly exemplifies that interaction between psychology and philosophy which he thought indispensable for the further development of either. For it is no mere inductive generalisation. Extensive observation of how men actually do respond to art is its 'realistic' groundwork. But these empirical facts are interpreted in the light of philosophical knowledge about the nature and function of the æsthetic mode.

Perhaps because it is an attempt to generalise about relations,

---

[1] *Ancient Art and Ritual*, Home University Library, 1913, pp. 127 ff.

[2] In an account of recent trends in English æsthetics ('Neuere Strömungen der angelsächsischen Ästhetik in ihrer Beziehung zur vergleichenden Literaturwissenschaft' in *Forschungsprobleme der Vergleichenden Literaturwissenschaft*, Tübingen, 1951) and earlier, before I knew how much it was part of his own intellectual heritage, in *Johann Elias Schlegel. A German Pioneer in Æsthetics*, Oxford, 1945, Chapter 3.

[3] *Æsthetic Letters*, XXV.

[4] In his review of Bürger's *Gedichte*, 1791: 'Aus der sanftern und fernenden Erinnerung mag er dichten.' The verb does not seem to have been assimilated into the German language. As has been shown by L. A. Willoughby ('Wordsworth and Germany', *Studies Presented to H. G. Fiedler*, Oxford, 1937, pp. 442-5), this may well have been the source, via Coleridge, of Wordsworth's famous phrase.

and changing relations (which is what he thought the generalisations of æsthetics must be about), the principle is not always
rightly understood, clearly worked out as it is in detail, simple in
ultimate formulation. He is concerned to allow for maximum
differentiations of response *in relation to* maximum differentiations
of the art forms which produce them, but *at the same time* to safeguard the æsthetic character of the relation. The interplay of two
sets of variables is already complex enough. But it is further com-
plicated by the immense range of æsthetic response which his
image of a sliding scale of distance provides for: at the one end
such remoteness that personal 'engagement' is insufficient to merit
the name of relation at all; at the other, the minimum distance
required for the relation to be called æsthetic, the limit beyond
which engagement topples over into involvement of a non-
æsthetic kind. This makes for a principle of immense flexibility.
But it demands a like flexibility in applying it. With what he calls
the antinomy of distance—'utmost decrease of distance without
its disappearance'—Bullough is not suggesting that 'there is only
*one* correct distance for each person and each thing', a statement
attributed to him by Professor L. A. Reid,[1] but which I cannot
find in the text either in so many words or by implication. He is
not setting up a practical norm at all. He is defining, in terms of his
own principle, the knife-edge character of 'ideal' æsthetic experience which, when it is most intensely and characteristically itself,
verges on loss of distance without ever losing it. The absolute
character of his statement is the absolute of theoretical definition.
To translate it into practical terms by introducing notions of
correctness for particular persons and things is to reverse the intention of his scale of distance, which allows for a whole range of
more or less distanced responses—even for a different distance
between the same person and the same thing on different occasions.

And it allows for the changing 'life' of a work of art as generation succeeds to generation. Hence the impropriety of invoking it,

---

[1] Op. cit., p. 56. Cf., too, *Lectures, infra*, p. 57, where Bullough describes the
kind of principle he was looking for.

as a critic recently did,[1] to prove that the practical character of Defoe's novels precludes their having been intended as art or being appreciated as such by us. This is to miss the point that the distancing hand of time may clear our relation of the practical interest a theme held for its author. And it is to locate the non-practical character of art where it does not belong, in the matter rather than the form. Anything whatsoever can become the subject of art, even the practical—so long as the artist's relation to this practicalness is filtered of its personal–practical appeal, which may happen willy-nilly and for all his overt practical intention. M. Rader[2] is misled in another way when he takes the antinomy of distance as a plea for lifelike art and so prints the essay next to excerpts from Ortega y Gasset as a foil to his defence of 'de-humanised' art. Bullough is not pleading for any particular kind of art at all. He is devising a principle which will explain variety of style, including the naturalistic—though the risks attendant on programmatic naturalism or programmatic formalism emerge clearly enough from his discussion. Finally it seems almost perverse to invoke psychical distance, as Rosamond Harding does,[3] to explain the time which must often elapse between a conception and the process of working it out. This is a feature of creative activity in general. *Psychical* distance has to do with artistic creation alone. And the whole point is that it must supervene *before* conception (with or without a lapse of time, which is in any case not the operative factor), that it is the very condition of artistic conception.

---

[1] Jonathan Bishop, 'Knowledge, Action and Interpretation in Defoe's Novels', *Journal of the History of Ideas*, 1952, 13, 1, p. 3. I am not, of course, suggesting that Bullough's principle is irrelevant to the problem. But, as Virginia Woolf says when contrasting Defoe with Emily Brontë: 'Reality is something they put at different distances' (*A Writer's Diary*, London, 1953, p. 83). The critic's task is to show at what distance, how and, perhaps, to suggest why.

[2] *A Modern Book of Æsthetics*, New York, 1935, 2nd ed., 1952.

[3] *An Anatomy of Inspiration*, Cambridge, 1942, p. 49.

Bullough's principle has remained an almost isolated pheno-menon in modern æsthetics. The state of the subject is still pretty much as he described it thirty-odd years ago: a mass of detailed observation and record with scant co-ordination, lacking in particular a *common stock* of accepted truths without which pro-gress in any study cannot be hoped for.[1] It is a fate shared by all the mental sciences, and the reason is doubtless to be sought outside and beyond any one of them, in the lack of an ade-quate conceptual framework. Æsthetics, at any rate, in the sense Bullough envisaged it, needs a new conception of mental-ity which can shed light on states of consciousness, instead of obscuring them as methods borrowed from the physical sciences have done.

One that he himself would have found both helpful and con-genial is Ernst Cassirer's definition of man as *animal symbolicum*,[2] constantly engaged in transforming experience into symbols, symbols which range from our primary sense-data to the sheerest abstractions of mathematics. In view of the ever increasing interest in symbol-using and symbol-reading, evident in the most diverse fields over the last thirty years, Susanne Langer has aptly called this 'the new key in philosophy'[3] and sees in it 'the most powerful generative idea in humanistic thinking today'.[4] By means of it she is able, on the one hand, to show that art, as one of the mind's symbolic transformations, is a rational activity; on the other, to solve the long-standing problem of the relation of art to feeling. For works of art, like any other symbols, are vehicles of *conception*. They enable us to conceive things inaccessible to discursive

---

[1] *Publications*, No. 8, p. 45.

[2] *An Essay on Man*, Yale University Press, 1944, p. 26. This book contains the gist of his pioneer work *Die Philosophie der symbolischen Formen*, 3 vols., Berlin, 1923–9.

[3] *Philosophy in a New Key*, Harvard University Press, 1942. Pelican Books Edition, New York, 1948.

[4] *Feeling and Form*, ed. cit., p. 22.

language, namely feeling. 'What art expresses is *not* actual feeling but ideas of feeling.'[1]

This development in philosophy would have enabled Bullough to transpose such important æsthetic principles as distance, or the interpenetration of mind and medium, out of the metaphorical into the conceptual mode. For he is not satisfied either with the common definition of art as an expression of feeling—unless this is so carefully qualified as to distinguish it from other, irrational, expressions such as a sigh or a symptom. He tackles the problem in the first essay he ever published[2] and insists that art is primarily formation (*Gestaltung*), the making of forms expressive of 'inward life'. And in his later work he is at pains to show that however much feeling is involved, it is feeling set before the eye of the mind, sufficiently removed to be contemplated. Through the formulation of it the artist himself discovers new meaning, and it is this meaning he exhibits to us. Such recognition of the interdependence of feeling and form positively begs for a theory of mind which accepts art as a means to knowledge and tells us what it makes known.

Nor is he content to be vague about that other catchword of æsthetics, intuition. He categorically rejects the idea that the intuitions of the artist come in disembodied form and only seek the body of the medium for the grossly practical purpose of their materialisation. On the contrary, his intuitions come in terms of his medium. This is indispensable for conception, not just a vehicle of communication. And to explain the mechanism of how mind can be permeated by something like paint, or stone, he draws on Arréat's notion of 'images de traduction'. But what are these, in effect, if not symbolic transformations of ordinary experience into artistic experience? They, too, await the insight that 'the medium is a type of symbolism'.[3] And once this is grasped,

---

[1] Ibid., p. 59. 'Ideas' may be misleading when the sentence is thus isolated. In the context of her argument it is perfectly clear.

[2] 'Matter and Form', *Publications*, No. 7.

[3] *Philosophy in a New Key*, Pelican Books Edition, p. 56.

the materiality of some artistic media presents no problem. For, as A. D. Ritchie puts it: 'It [mental life] is mental not because the symbols are immaterial, for they are often material perhaps always material, but because they are symbols.'[1]

And if medium permeates mind, mind transforms medium, discerning æsthetic possibilities in its 'givenness' (whether it be given by nature or, as in the case of language, already a highly organised form which is nevertheless taken as raw material by the artist). To elucidate this other direction in the two-way process Bullough has recourse to Adolf Hildebrand's distinction between the structural and the spatial forms in the plastic arts (a distinction which Mrs. Langer has taken up, too, and brilliantly elaborated). What the artist aims at producing by the manipulation of his material forms are the optical spatial illusions which are his æsthetic forms. In recognising that this applies *mutatis mutandis* to all the arts Bullough is surely on the verge of seeing that art might be defined in terms of æsthetic illusion, an illusion brought about by the symbolic transformation of the elements of the medium into a unity of a different order.

There is no call for surprise at this closeness of thought. Both writers stem from the same æsthetic tradition. It might be called the tradition of centrality; and its spokesmen have more often been articulate artists than professional philosophers. The former have always intuitively known that the either-or positions of the latter—mind *or* body, thought *or* feeling, spirit *or* matter—did not fit the facts of the artistic case. They knew that art involved the whole man. They felt they were bringers of news, and news inaccessible except through their medium. But it is just this crucial problem of medium, as J. M. Thorburn complained,[2] that has been so cavalierly treated by philosophers. Either they have ignored it altogether or they have roundly asserted that there can be no such thing. With the passing of the 'ghost in the machine'

---

[1] *The Natural History of Mind*, London, 1936, pp. 279.

[2] *Art and the Unconscious*, London, 1925, p. 37. Thorburn develops Bullough's principle of distance in a highly suggestive way.

view of mind, and the extension of 'mental' activity to include the movements and perceptions of the body as well as the goings-on in the head, they should be in a fair position to mend their ways. In which case a good deal of æsthetics—and criticism—will have to be rewritten.

\*　　\*　　\*

Bullough's *Lectures* take us to the point where æsthetics hands over to philosophy. He distinguishes the various modes of consciousness—practical, scientific, ethical, æsthetic[1]—without, however, suggesting how they might be co-ordinated. It is evident that he rates the æsthetic highest, as the mode in which imagination is at full stretch, and without whose revivifying power we become narrowly inflexible in mind and heart. Are we, then, to infer that he deemed it capable of being the integrating principle?

For the answer to this question we must look to an essay[2] which is not chiefly on æsthetics and not, therefore, reprinted here. In it he reviews the claims of each mode to be the dominant ideal which might unify our fragmented culture, and rejects them all— even the æsthetic: 'It has a great attraction for cultivated minds. . . . It is an essentially human ideal. Unfortunately it cannot get beyond its own confines, and ceases to be æsthetic as soon as it attempts to do so: the contact with realities degrades it almost at once into sheer sensationalism and moral paganism of a peculiarly perverse kind.'[3]

This is true; though he ought to have pointed out that the greatest advocates of education through art have seen the danger quite clearly. Schiller rigorously defined the boundaries of the æsthetic, and showed how its infinite power to restore us briefly to a state of indeterminate freedom and full potentiality is dependent on its utter powerlessness to effect specific results of thought,

[1]  His indebtedness to Schiller is again evident.
[2]  'The Relation of Literature and the Arts', *Publications*, No. 20.
[3]  Ibid., p. 111.

deed or judgment.[1] Goethe, even more bluntly outspoken about
its impotence in any sphere but its own, was also more lucidly
aware of the dark face of this as of any other human good. The
state of indifferency, requisite and sanctioned in the moment of
æsthetic grace, degenerates if held on to when determinate states
are called for into indifferentism and worse. 'The middle, that is
the indifferent, states are for a god or a beast. Hate or love, victory
or death, tyranny or submission, these are for man. . . . Neutrality
and impartiality are but absolute tyranny in disguise.'[2] And it was,
after all, the arch-æsthete, Oscar Wilde, who provided us with the
cautionary tale about such transgression of frontiers, allegorising
the appalling metamorphosis of æsthete into beast by letting his
hero arrogate to himself the serene immutability which is the
privilege of art alone, while his portrait bears the burden of his
days.

The only way of integrating the various modes, Bullough
maintained, is by a principle outside and above them all. He himself found this in religion. Not all of us can or would wish to
follow him here—though if we accept the suggestion of some
scholars about the etymology of the word ('relegere: to gather
together, collect, ponder over'), it is no bad term for that point of
recollection and conviction from which, with varying prompt-
ness, we survey the kinds of response at our disposal, not for the
purpose of ordering them in a static and abstractive hierarchy, but
for judging in a concrete situation which of them might fittingly
predominate. And to seek the integrative principle at a higher
level than the elements to be integrated is in itself sound. We find
Bullough doing it often inside his æsthetic writings—when he
speaks of the artist ruthlessly subordinating his sensuous delight in

---

[1]  Dr. Ilse Appelbaum argues convincingly that in his tragedies Schiller shows
the disastrous consequences of trying to persist inappropriately in the state of
æsthetic freedom (*Schiller's View of Tragedy in the Light of his Æsthetic.*
Thesis submitted for the Degree of Ph.D. in the University of London,
1952).

[2]  Goethe, in conversation with Riemer, September, 1809.

his medium, along with other elements of his experience, to the higher interest of his vision, or of our natural interest in technique being subordinated in æsthetic response to contemplation of the work as a whole. This same principle now enables him to set limits to the æsthetic mode, *not* by curtailing its legitimate sphere of action, or exhorting us to surrender to it only with reserve, or importing into it standards from the co-ordinate modes; but by distinguishing it as strictly as may be[1] and then seeking a higher view-point from which to discover how it may live in concord with the others.

He was under no illusions that this was easy, either for the individual or the community: 'with any degree of cultural complexity such an internal correlation of the various aspects of culture becomes a matter of difficulty.'[2] But, unlike many who concern themselves with this problem, he succumbed neither to regressive impulses nor to the security wish of over-simplification. He may deplore a lost cultural unity. But his historical sense taught him that this has been achieved but rarely and for brief periods, and preserved him from presenting such equilibrium as the norm from which our own age has exceptionally fallen. It made him sceptical too of deliberate attempts to impose it, to take past integrations as models for present guidance, to 'romanticise' either art or culture back into union and a common appeal. For to do this would mean amputating some manifestations of human life and, in his view, only all the potentialities of human nature, '*together and in co-ordination*', constitute culture. Here, as much as anywhere in his work, we find what is easily the most distinguishing mark of his mind: the balance of two equally strong impulses, one towards differentiation and the other towards unity. His aim is always clarity with richness.                    E. M. W.

---

[1] It would never occur to him, as it does to some, to confuse æsthetic with mystical contemplation. The aim of the former is to apprehend meaning immanent in forms; of the latter, surely, to transcend phenomena altogether.

[2] *Publications*, No. 20, p. 109.

# The Modern Conception of Æsthetics

A COURSE OF LECTURES
DELIVERED AUTUMN 1907
IN THE UNIVERSITY OF
CAMBRIDGE

Ενεργείᾳ ἔσμεν. ARISTOTLE

'Vom Nützlichen durchs Wahre zum Schönen.'

GOETHE

'Philosophy serves culture, not by the fancied gift of
absolute or transcendental knowledge, but by suggesting
questions which help one to detect the passion, and strangeness, and dramatic contrasts of life.'

W. PATER *Renaissance Studies*

# I

To embrace all sides of so vast a study as Æsthetics has become at the present day requires almost a life-time of labour and treasures of personal experience of which I unfortunately cannot boast. Nor would it even be possible to compress its various aspects into one course of lectures. My intention is rather to convey a general idea of what, in the light of modern thought, science and speculation, Æsthetics has come to mean, to present an account of the principal problems which have recently been raised and to indicate what phase of development their discussion has at present reached. More particularly in Germany and France, and quite lately also in America and Italy, Æsthetics has become a study to which some of the leading intellects have devoted their best efforts and a large share of their time, while England, except for stray moments and in some exceptional individuals, has generally stood aloof from it. It is true, of course, that, in Germany especially, Æsthetics can look back to a relatively long chain of development. Starting with Baumgarten's *Æsthetica* in 1750, it can boast of such names as Kant, Fichte, Hegel, Schelling, Solger, Weisse, and other Metaphysicians, side by side with men who approached its problems from the practical or theoretical artistic side, such as Winckelmann, Lessing, Goethe, Schiller, Sulzer, or still later Gottfried Semper, and quite recently Adolf Hildebrand or Johannes Schilling. And yet we can with every show of reason assert that Æsthetics in the modern sense of the term is still in its infancy. The fact is that the chain of development dating from the eighteenth century has been broken, and broken quite recently. Instead of being a department of Metaphysics, as it had been, Æsthetics has endeavoured with the help, though also against the will of Psychology in its present form, to occupy autonomously its own ground and to stand upon its own legs. This move goes back to Fechner who, in his *Vorschule der Æsthetik* (1876), tried to give it a psychological-scientific basis; and though the controversy between Æsthetics, Psychology and Philosophy still continues, the first has at least made considerable progress towards independence and autonomy within its own sphere. Fresh suggestions, new points of view for attacking its problems, new theories concerning its demarcation against other, already firmly established studies such as Physiology or Ethics, or frontier-disputes with studies only lately risen in prominence, such as Psychology, Sociology or the science of Religions, are constantly brought to light. Even the settlement of its own scope and of the spheres falling within its purview cannot, strictly speaking, be considered final. Æsthetics is still evolving, even with amazing rapidity; books written thirty, twenty, even ten years ago, are in many points already obsolete—such has been its quickened growth under the impulse especially of Psychology. It is evident that under these conditions it would be unprofitable, if not impossible, to try to force it for good and all into a definitely fixed system, even if my competence were sufficient for such a Procrustes-task.

Apart from this purely theoretical purpose I secretly cherish a hope of a more general and practical kind. Almost everyone is interested in Art, if not from an abstract point of view, at least as a rational being who, experiencing certain effects, would also like to explain them to himself. Art-speculation forms a stock-in-trade of ordinary educated conversation; and the hope I entertain is that by presenting to you an account of æsthetic problems in their wider formulation, this self-scrutiny and the exchange of opinion based upon it may be stimulated and its tools refined. Not infrequently in the course of conversation problems are raised as great novelties, and solutions suggested which are supposed to enlighten the situation with freshly-discovered rays of knowledge, but which are in fact ludicrously obsolete and out-of-date. A kind of touchiness in matters of art and its effects, and a consequent asperity in the discussion of them, are likewise due to dogmatic ignorance of the widely divergent ways of enjoying art. An account of present developments in Æsthetics may, I believe, help to remedy such defects. It may show the need for care in handling such a fragile fabric as artistic enjoyment, and add a more discriminating touch to the pleasures of exploration in one's own self.

It follows from these remarks that these lectures are intended merely as a ramble through the field of Æsthetics, not as a thorough survey over its domain. And if you miss in them the strict coherence of a complete and self-consistent system, I beg you to remember that they are only an Introduction. For convenience sake, however, I shall endeavour to thread the most important problems upon a continuous line of thought running throughout the whole length of the course.

In view of the fact that Æsthetics is a new study here, I shall assume, though it may be contrary to fact, that the term evokes either no meaning at all, or at least a very indefinite and hazy meaning, and I shall discuss its significance from points of view which may to some extent appear elementary. I shall attempt to give the term a more precise sense first in a negative and then in a positive form.

If we lived in the eighteenth century we might, perhaps, entitle the subject 'a philosophical inquiry into the origin of our ideas of the Beautiful' after Burke's grandiose title of his famous treatise. Even to call it a 'theory of taste' would be less prosaic and more expressive to the majority of people than the 'study of Æsthetics'. Yet Æsthetics is not exactly either the one or the other, though in its full sense it ought to include both. It is undoubtedly true that the word staggers people at first and makes them shy, as an unknown but formidable-looking object startles a horse. But if I could succeed in making clear all that it implies, how much purely human interest is concentrated in it, and how little abstract and abstruse speculation it contains, Æsthetics might, without losing anything of its comprehensive vastness, be brought humanly near to you and evoke an infinitely larger sympathy in your minds than either a 'Theory of Taste' or 'An inquiry into the origin of our ideas of the Beautiful' could possibly engender.

Æsthetics is, as I said, a most indefinite thing to the majority of people. It means little to them, and the little meaning it does possess is regarded with suspicion. At the same time, to some it appears to borrow from Art a reflected glory, to be surrounded with some of its joyous freedom and exquisite refinement. The peculiar, idealistic atmosphere surrounding Art and impregnating such studies as deal with it, clings also in some measure to Æsthetics. On the other hand, the languid interest in art entertained by other people necessarily detracts too from the sympathy shown to Æsthetics. Thus it has come to form a centre round which a number of dim associations, both agreeable and disagreeable, have crystallised. Unfortunately it can, like Metaphysics and Ethics, Physics and Mathematics, boast of the formidable ending in -ics, and consequently appears to many a curious hybrid between Philosophy and Science. Its metaphysical ancestry seems to point to exclusively philosophical speculations on, perhaps, transcendental matters, such as the metaphysical relation of the true: good: beautiful. It is considerably humanised, if called a 'Theory of Taste'. But then, what is 'Taste'? Theories of Taste have the dogmatic habit of taking so much for granted! They play with 'good' and 'bad taste', with 'Beauty', with 'Perfection', 'Harmony' and 'Art', as if all these things were balls, light, round, self-complete, unattached, even hollow; while everyone feels that they are in fact replete with meanings, weighed down with individual associations and planted with numberless ramified roots in the ground of concrete human experience. Again, Æsthetics reminds one of 'Æstheticism' with its sham-refinement and general morbidness, of consumptive-looking women with amazed, dreamy eyes, in flowing robes of weird colours, aimlessly holding long-stalked lilies in nervous, ivory-white, thin-tipped fingers; of fierce-faced men in velvet jackets with long bow-ties flowing in the wind, who seem to express their inward artisticness by outward dilapidation and to combine a spiritual hyper-aristocracy with socialistic, almost anarchical, appearances; of an atmosphere heavy with overpowering exotic scent, effeminate

finickingness and general decadence. If, instead of vague reminiscences we connect a more definite idea with Æsthetics, it means to
so-called 'practical' people talking about something which may,
no doubt, give a more or less refined pleasure, but, after all, only
'pleasure', i.e. something which is strictly speaking superfluous and
a mere luxury, namely Art. It is, of course, true that to be *really*
practical the necessity of pleasure must be admitted. But if
Æsthetics is further defined as the attempt to make theories about
this pleasure, its legitimacy may all the more be called in question:
for what is the use of making theories about enjoyment? Such useless pedantry only destroys the amusement that Art might otherwise afford.

These, I imagine, are some of the hazy features which Æsthetics
usually presents. They contain in germ some of the great arguments which are often advanced against it, and I shall discuss these
in a more precise formulation in order to circumscribe *negatively*
its modern conception by showing what Æsthetics is not. These
arguments differ widely from each other in value and weight.
They might, in general, be divided into more popular and more
theoretical arguments, though, in their indefiniteness, they mostly
retain a popular tinge.

## I. POPULAR OBJECTIONS

1. The first objection is almost bœotian in its unmitigated
crudity. Yet it is exceedingly popular, both in the sense of being
widely-spread and of being unphilosophical in the highest degree.
It is even, like most childish arguments, to some extent irrefutable.
To condense all its many indefinite meanings into a concise form,
it may be taken to state that *Æsthetics is an altogether useless and
highly unpractical study*. There is not the faintest shadow of use or
general benefit in trying to find principles of, or make theories
about, Art, or to explain why the Beautiful *is* beautiful or why one
enjoys a good picture or goes to see a fine play. Has ever a life been
saved, or a discovery been made, or a fortune accumulated or the

fame of a nation been spread by occupation with Æsthetics? No. Have men been morally improved or their conduct been influenced towards the Better by Æsthetics? No. Has ever a man produced a finer painting or built a better house or written a more fascinating book, because he studied Æsthetics? No, on the contrary; Æstheticians themselves insist upon the antagonism between artistic execution and æsthetic speculation. Did not Leonardo da Vinci himself emphasise this incompatibility? And if anyone knew it, he did. Then what is the use of Æsthetics except as an intellectual pastime or semi-philosophical amusement?

2. The second objection is more refined, since it makes some concessions to philosophic susceptibilities, in not denying wholesale their ideal of 'knowledge for knowledge's sake'. It leaves the question of usefulness aside, and attacks instead its possibility. 'There is no accounting for tastes' is its corner-stone, whatever other façades it may present. Its foundation is the belief that *it is impossible to build any theory upon anything so unstable, notoriously shifting and admittedly relative as pleasure and displeasure.* Again the formulation is lax and indefinite. I will try to give its various meanings a more precise shape.

That great cynic La Rochefoucauld said in one of his *Maximes*[1]: 'Notre amour-propre souffre plus impatiemment la condamnation de nos goûts que de nos opinions.' Why? Because our opinions, acquired by education and experience, can be altered, but our tastes are innate. As poets are born not made, so our taste is a gift of nature not a matter of voluntary acquirement. To possess good taste is as much an accident as to possess bad taste, and neither the one nor the other can be modified by theoretical knowledge or improved by abstract instruction. Both the one and the other are legitimate by reason of their spontaneous origin, and to condemn the one or praise the other is as unjust as to establish a theory upon the verdict of 'good' taste to the neglect and detriment of his less favoured brother.

[1] *Max.* xiii.

The well-known *lack of consensus of opinion* in matters of Art is another form of the same argument which is perhaps more frequently advanced against Æsthetics. For it is a matter of daily experience that no two persons derive the same pleasure from a work of art, nor is it possible to demonstrate by intellectual reasoning the correctness of good taste, or the failure of bad taste to appreciate the beauties which good taste discerns in a work. Altogether appreciation is merely a matter of fashion and imitation, conscious and unconscious. Anatole France recently gave strong expression to his disbelief in Æsthetics on this ground: 'Pour fonder la critique, on parle de tradition et de consentement universel. Il n'y en a pas. L'opinion presque générale, il est vrai, favorise certaines œuvres. Mais c'est en vertu d'un préjugé, et nullement par choix et par effet d'une préférence spontanée. Les œuvres que tout le monde admire sont celles que personne n'examine.'[1]

In reality, few people have the courage of their opinion in matters of art. The verdict of the connoisseur is too authoritative; disagreement and the feeling of shame too painful. At any rate to find fault gives an air of connoisseurship, while to admire exposes us to the danger of humiliating contradiction. Even the knowledge that whatever side one takes one will never be alone, is little comfort, for we naturally prefer to be on the side of the connoisseur than to be classed with naïvely-admiring blockheads. Thus to appeal to the majority in matters æsthetic is unsafe, since its verdict is vitiated by insincere or unconsciously imitated judgments. Bismarck may have been right with his bitter remark that the minority is always right. But what guarantee is there that the opinion of the select few is better than that of the many?

Again, Æsthetics professes to state the principle of Beauty. If this deserves the name of principle it should hold good always and in all cases. A principle of scientific value admits of no exceptions. But whatever definition of Beauty you may take, it is easy to produce instances where it either does not apply, or is even flatly con-

---

[1] *Le Jardin d'Epicure*, Paris, 1895, p. 219.

tradicted by the general verdict, or becomes to such an extent abstract that it is concretely perfectly meaningless. The lack of consensus of opinion has invariably proved fatal to the establishment of any one æsthetic principle.

3. The third objection penetrates even beyond such externalities as the lack of consensus. It lays stress upon the psychological aspect of the matter and enlists sentimental or largely emotional arguments in its service. It is raised in particular by people who are greatly devoted to Art and especially sensitive to artistic effects; and it is all the more discouraging to the student of Æsthetics to find just those whom he would expect to be his natural allies in the ranks of his most obstinate enemies.

The enthusiasm of art-lovers, amateurs in the best sense of the word, and of artists themselves has unfortunately always made them suspicious, even openly hostile to Æsthetics. For they constantly complain of its attempt to impose rules. It is difficult to know what exactly is meant by this. But it seems that the endeavour to systematise anything of so free and playful a nature as art-effects appears to them an absurdity, if not a piece of insolent pedantry. Even worse than that: they resent not merely the systematisation, but the scientific curiosity. The desire for intellectual knowledge appears, if directed towards phenomena and facts which they themselves feel to be a mystery, a blasphemy almost, certainly an impertinent intrusion into the sanctum of their own most intimate personality. Their susceptibility to art makes them realise the impossibility of forcing (as they imagine) the endless variety of effects in their minutest shadings under one rigid rule of thumb. Their reverence for art, the living connection they feel between it and their own self, the purely personal elements involved in the effects and in the production of art, all combine to produce a half-angry, half-contemptuous attitude towards Æsthetics. To submit their artistic fancies, their artistic impressions, their æsthetic ideals to an external authority which pretends to legislate, is all the more unbearable when this professes to be scientific, i.e. abstractly intellectual.

This is an objection which in a theoretical formulation we shall meet again presently.

So far the popular objections. The theoretical arguments against Æsthetics increase in subtlety and technical niceties.

## II. THEORETICAL OBJECTIONS

1. The first objection of this theoretical order is in particular the argument of scientists and other positivistically or materialistically inclined people. It endeavours to discredit Æsthetics by attacking Art, by denying to it any objective foundation. Of course the existence of works of art as objectively existing things of reality cannot be argued away. But (and this is a good instance of the usual sledge-hammer arguments in æsthetic matters) do not æstheticians themselves admit that the *æsthetic* aspect of a work of art is not identical with its *material* aspect? A block of marble may be an objective reality. But when we see in it a Hermes or a Venus, we profess to see something which is *not* objectively there, but which we subjectively (how, makes no matter) interpret into it by the play of our imagination with this block of stone. A painting is objectively a surface of canvas blotted with patches of colours. But if we see in it a landscape suffused with moonlight or quivering in the heat of a summer's day or hidden in the steaming mists of an autumn morning, this may be a very pretty fancy, but it is only fancy, not an objective reality. For how can a piece of canvas be objectively a face or a landscape? Is this not sadly like the aimless amusement of idle moments: seeing faces in the fire?

Again, æsthetic effects are confessedly purely subjective. Worse than that; they are often predominantly emotional. The raptures of a symphony, the bitterness of tragedy, the delights of an idyllic poem are all only subjective mental conditions. It is true that real anger, genuine sorrow are subjective states too; but the *æsthetic* subjective states cannot even claim the basis of objective facts and reality to which emotional and other subjective states of ordinary life can point as proofs of their genuineness. For æsthetic emotions are *illusions*, and illusions are notoriously false. They are the contradiction of objective reality, they are lies which we consciously accept. Thus Art and Art-effects are not only false, they are also immoral. The consent we accord them only increases the immorality of playing with such illusions. That Art is a 'conscious self-deception'—whatever that may mean—is not only the gist of a recent æsthetic theory, but also the scientific, positivist conception of æsthetic effects.[1]

When considered from the side of the artist, Art hardly fares any better before such a scientific Rhadamanthus. Imagination, which plays so large a part in artistic production, and which in the popular semi-scientific mind is almost equivalent to romancing or idle fancies, appears dangerously akin to morbid conditions, dreams, hysterical states, hallucinations, obsessions, fixed ideas. The complete loss of himself, the involuntary impulse working in the producing artist, these are things which cannot but be viewed with profoundest suspicion. Poets may euphemistically be called prophets or seers; in reality they are but dreamers. Is it not generally admitted that genius is a kind of insanity? Is science not satisfied, now that Lombroso has described geniuses as belonging to the large class of 'hystero–epileptic degenerates'?[2]

How can a serious, scientific study be made of, or principles be established for, such a phantastic concoction of unrealities?

2. The next objection is the theoretical version of the last but one. Let us waive the previous materialistic argument. We have then to admit that æsthetic effects are largely emotional; they are not a purely intellectual experience. But, if this is conceded, then it must also be admitted that it is impossible to rationalise it, to comprehend merely by the intellect and the reason, phenomena

---

[1] Cf. K. Lange, *Das Wesen der Kunst*, 2 vols., Berlin, 1901. F. Paulhan, *Le Mensonge de l'Art*, Paris, 1907.

[2] If this argument appear as formulated by me *ad hoc*, it should be remembered that Socrates used it before me to prove precisely the same point (*Ion*, 533d–536d). Cf. O. Külpe, 'Anfänge der psychol. Æsthetik bei den Griechen', *Philosophische Abhandlungen*, Berlin, 1906, p. 115.

which, by their very nature, lie outside the sphere of reason.

In order to spare myself the reproach of manufacturing my own arguments against the position I wish to defend, I may perhaps be allowed to quote a passage from a review of a recent American book on Æsthetics, which is made the occasion for a vigorous attack on Æsthetics generally.[1]

'A definition of Beauty', says the author of this review, 'is an attempt to understand beauty by means of the intellect alone. But since our experience of beautiful things is not purely intellectual, we cannot express that experience in purely intellectual terms. No amount of hard thinking will enable a man to know a good picture from a bad one, any more than it will enable a man to become a good painter. Hard thinking is, of course, necessary for both the understanding and the consummate practice of the arts. But a work of art is produced, like an action, by the whole of a man's faculties and not by his intellect alone. And so we can understand it only by the use of all our faculties. But it is only by an understanding of particular works of art that we can come to know and feel what art is, and when we have reached that knowledge and feeling we can no more express it in terms of pure reason than we can express the content of one of Beethoven's Symphonies in terms of pure reason. *This, I know, implies that all Æsthetics expressed in terms of pure reason are futile. But surely experience shows that they are.* You have only to read the first part of Tolstoy's *What is Art?* in which he knocks over all existing theories like nine-pins, and still more the second part in which he builds up a theory of his own just as easily destructible, to be convinced that no existing theories cover the facts.'

There is nothing to be added to these sentences. They leave little to be desired in clear and forcible condemnation of all Æsthetics.

3. This brings us to the last objection, whose line of attack is not dissimilar to the previous one, though its spirit is less virulent and

[1] Review of G. L. Raymond, *The Essentials of Æsthetics* (London, 1907) by A. Clutton-Brock in *Tribune*, 1 March 1907.

its formulation more elegant. Its pith is the impossibility and use-lessness of a definition of Beauty based on abstract principles to account for the fullness and multiplicity of æsthetic experiences. As representative let me choose Walter Pater who, in the Preface to *The Renaissance*, formulates the argument with his usual grace and precision: 'Many attempts', he says, 'have been made by writers on Art and Poetry to define Beauty in the abstract, to ex-press it in the most general terms, to find some universal formula for it. The value of these attempts has most often been in the suggestive and penetrating things said by the way. Such discus-sions help us very little to enjoy what has been well done in art or poetry, to discriminate between what is more and what is less excellent in them, or to use words like beauty, excellence, art, poetry, with a more precise meaning·than they would otherwise have. Beauty, like all other qualities presented to human experi-ence, is relative; and the definition of it becomes unmeaning and useless in proportion to its abstractness. To define beauty, not in the most abstract but in the most concrete terms possible, to find, not its universal formula, but the formula which expresses most adequately this or that special manifestation of it, is the aim of the true student of Æsthetics.'

Even without possessing Pater's marvellous æsthetic sensitive-ness or the stores of knowledge which he brought to a work of art, the strings of memories and reminiscences which he could set vibrating in his contemplation of individual works, anyone who is capable of any artistic appreciation must subscribe to his indict-ment. This objection, like the last one, or like the third popular objection, is essentially representative of the attitude of the Art-lover towards, or rather against, Æsthetics: the same resentment against scientific pedantry, the same disbelief in the omnipotence of abstract speculation, the same scorn for 'rules', definitions, and formulae.

For the present these objections may suffice. I think they repre-sent fairly accurately the mental attitude of various classes of individuals towards Æsthetics. I know that there are other objections of a different nature and of a still more abstractly theoretical kind, which attack not so much the possibility or use of Æsthetics, as its autonomy and right of existence as an independent study within the constituted world of thought. These attacks are mainly due to methodological considerations and will find their place in the discussion of the relationship of Æsthetics to Ethics, Psychology, Sociology, etc.

————

I shall now endeavour to make answer to these objections, not so much with the intention of completely disproving them (which might lead too far afield), as in the hope that, as starting points of discussion, they may help to make clearer the modern conception of Æsthetics.

To I. 1. There is little doubt that Æsthetics is useless in the sense that it does not in any direct or practical manner benefit humanity in its material welfare, though even this point, if specially pressed, might be defended with some hope of success. Under the circumstances little time need be wasted with proof or disproof of this fact. In the usual sense of the term 'practical usefulness' it is fairly self-evident. It should, nevertheless, be noted that a detailed discussion of this question must at once lead to the broader issues of the usefulness or uselessness of preoccupation with theoretical problems in general and of its bearing upon human culture and development. The remark which so profoundly astounded Harpagon: 'il faut manger pour vivre, et non pas vivre pour manger', belongs essentially to the same order of problems. The use or lack of use of anything is not necessarily decided by an appeal to its bearing upon material improvements of existence. Not only Æsthetics, studies such as Ethics and Metaphysics are open to exactly the same criticism, although as a rule no one thinks of attacking these on grounds of their practical uselessness. But, it is interesting to reflect, Ethics, or Moral Philosophy, has generally been more exempt from this reproach than either Metaphysics or Æsthetics. On account of its supposed bearing upon human conduct it seems to be in more direct contact with human life and welfare. Metaphysics, on the other hand, makes no secret of its barrenness in practical results; and if Æsthetics were in exactly the same case, there would, I think, be no need to make any secret of it on its part either. But Æsthetics can, it seems to me, claim an infinitely closer relationship to concrete life than Metaphysics. It is true, of course, that it does not fit a man to build bridges, discover antiseptic treatment, invent wireless telegraphy or solve the problems of aerial flight. Its utility lies neither in the material nor the social sphere; it is necessarily confined to purely personal results. But just as the rank popularly assigned to Ethics is due to the importance attached to moral conduct in human affairs, so our conception of the subject matter of Æsthetics necessarily influences our estimate of the study itself. That is to say, it is the value we attach to Art which raises or lowers the value of Æsthetics in this particular respect. If Art is put on the same plane as culinary practice, Æsthetics could not claim the importance of a cookery-book. But if it is held to be an essential factor in human life, one of the principal manifestations of the human mind and the concrete expression of human experience, then the theoretical study of such an activity, of such a manifestation of spiritual life and agency, may aspire to equal consideration with other highly-assessed theoretical occupations. Thus one aspect of this problem of Æsthetics as a theoretical study leads to general problems of culture; the other aspect brings us face to face with the question of the Function of Art, with which I hope to deal later. The general character of this first objection hardly deserves a more extended answer than the few suggestions I have thrown out.

To I. 2. The answer to the second objection leads us further into the heart of Æsthetics, to its psychological aspect. This argument urges the impossibility of accounting for tastes, and insists that, in all their shiftiness and relativity, they are incapable of affording a sound substructure to æsthetic theories. But the objection makes a twofold mistake: first in believing that tastes cannot be accounted for, and secondly in thinking that a consensus of opinion is required as a foundation of Æsthetics.

That there are differences of taste is undeniable, in spite of the many attempts that have been made to represent them as something superficial and non-existent. Less undeniable is the assertion that it is impossible to account for them. It seems to be one of the many survivals of the old 'faculty-psychology' to speak of taste, good and bad, of pleasure or displeasure, of intellect, emotion, and will, as if the human mind were a chest of drawers, each drawer labelled with its contents and to be opened or shut at will without thereby interfering with any other drawer and *its* contents. To keep to the simile, it might with better advantage be likened to a wardrobe in which, by opening its doors, the entire contents are displayed, though we may then direct our attention to this or that individual shelf in it. In other words, the misconception lies in imagining that all these separately labelled departments, those things we call pleasure or taste or intellect or will, etc., are isolated facts of experience; or even in regarding them as simple facts at all. Each concrete pleasure, each concrete volitional act, is more than merely a pleasing state of consciousness or a manifestation of our will. Its whole intellectual, emotional, even sensational background or setting forms part and parcel of it, however much we may in abstract language ignore this setting in order to direct our attention solely to the pleasure or the act of will. And 'taste' too is a merely verbal entity, an abstraction to which nothing of a simple nature corresponds in our psychic life. We may make elegant definitions of it and say, for instance, that 'taste is our faculty of appreciation'.[1] But this explains nothing whatever, for it makes 'taste' clear only by crowding all the difficulties and intricacies into 'appreciation'. What *is* appreciation? There lies the difficulty.

---

[1] Addison, for instance, defines taste as 'that faculty of the sou *l* which discerns the beauties of an author with pleasure, and the imperfections with dislike' (*The Spectator*, No. 409). This is really supposed to be a definition of 'good' taste, not of taste generally.

Under the word 'appreciation' lie hidden precisely all the complexities of the psychic setting itself, which link 'taste' to our conscious life and make it, not a simple detached phenomenon, but a fact of our consciousness and experience. Taste, in the sense in which it is used in the proverb, is not a faculty, but *this experience itself*, namely our manner of being psychically affected by certain conditions or stimulations; or, to use a convenient psychological term, it is a form of 're-action'. A is affected by a certain picture in one way, B in another; *A's* mode of behaviour, or his reaction, constitutes his taste, which differs more or less widely from *B's*, and in so far as A is *in the habit* of being affected by this kind of picture in this particular way we say that A has good taste, while the habitual form of reaction of B is considered as bad taste. The factors which tend to form *A's* mode of reaction so as to render it relatively constant are, naturally, exceedingly complex and comprise such things as natural temperament, breeding, habit, education, example, and imitation, and spontaneous modifications through knowledge or reflexion. Neither is taste anything absolutely fixed but, as we all know, liable to fluctuations; nor is it a reaction which takes place invariably and in all directions in the same way. In other words, not only do the tastes of individuals differ; the taste of the same individual differs at different times and under different forms of stimulation. Taste may be highly developed and refined in some respects and more or less crude in others. Tastes differ not only in goodness and badness, but also in fullness and poorness, simplicity and nicety of differentiation and in degrees of development.

This may appear to make taste all the more *un*accountable. But a thing, it must be noted, is only unaccountable if the causes or factors leading to its existence are unknowable. In this case, however, we have causes and factors in plenty. It is true, of course, that these causes are not ultimate, that we can point to no cause to explain why my temperament or psychic constitution, by reason of which my taste is this particular, individual taste, is such as it is. Even hereditary influences only beg the question. Still taste, as a more or less habitual form of reaction or behaviour, as a relatively constant mode of experience, has antecedents which do account for it, as far as scientific explanation does account for anything. The *efficient* causes are mostly known to us and, inasmuch as they are known, there *is* an accounting for taste. And we certainly do account for taste in ordinary life often enough. We have a perfectly definite idea *why* X dislikes Chopin or Y paintings of the Dutch School. We regard it as perfectly feasible to explain why a Red Indian should not appreciate a play by Pinero, or a Bushman a Gothic cathedral. And not only do we believe in practically accounting for such individual or racial differences of taste; divergences in the collective taste of certain periods also appear intelligible. We can point to very definite reasons to explain the aversion of the Louis XVI period to Gothic architecture, the lower appreciation of Homer compared to that of Virgil in the Italian Renaissance, the varying appreciation of Greek Art in the Quattrocento, in the time of Louis XIV and among the modern 'Parnassiens', or the different attitudes to the Middle Ages in the Romantic Movement and at the present day.

The lack of consensus of opinion in æsthetic matters is consequently not unaccountable. It is a fact which is a cause neither for surprise, nor even for regret. And far from denying this lack of consensus, or requiring any consensus for its foundation, modern Æsthetics takes it as part of its field of study. It is one of its problems to trace the remote and complex causes of the differences of appreciation, in the individual, in races and in various historical periods, with the help of Psychology, Ethnology, Sociology, and History.

All this will probably be conceded. And yet there is a lurking suspicion in the mind that the matter of 'Taste' has not been exhausted by showing that tastes have antecedents which may account for them, and by stating that a consensus of opinion is not required for Æsthetics. Let us remember the spirit in which the proverb is generally applied to a concrete case of a difference of opinion. It states the differences of tastes *not* in the impartial spirit of scientific tolerance towards facts objectively to be investigated. It implies rather a spirit of half-angry, half-contemptuous intolerance, half-patronising pity, half-impatient animosity. In the proverb it is not only a question of the differences of tastes, but of the particular difference between *good* and *bad* taste. This is the real pith of the objection. Æsthetics is objected to, because it presumes to make this distinction and because it ventures to make pronouncements on the basis of its theories.

If I have gauged this objection aright, it seems to me that the differences between this and the third objection practically disappear and that the two are fused into one.

To I. 3. The main difficulty of countering this objection lies in the fact that it is less a reasoned argument against Æsthetics than the expression of an instinctive aversion against an authority which is supposed to be foreign to Art. 'Le cœur a ses raisons que la raison ne connaît pas', i.e. it is notoriously useless to adduce reasoned statements to overcome emotional resistance. As far as it is possible to discern its meaning and to formulate it, however vaguely, this objection appears to imply that Æsthetics lays down regulations, concerning both art-production and art-effect, which ought to be considered as binding by the artist as well as by the recipient; that Æsthetics, in other words, prescribes certain rules which a work of art ought to fulfil, or which the spectator ought to observe in order to obtain the proper impression. Nothing would indeed be more natural than that both artist and spectator should resent such interference from an alien and abstract authority. The objection generally appeals successfully to our sense of freedom and independence in such a matter as Art.

Merely to state in return that all this is a false alarm, that Æsthetics is quite innocent of such attempts upon individual liberty and that the objection most probably rests upon a misconception, is hardly a sufficient answer, especially as Æsthetics cannot completely abdicate its authority, by whatever misconstruction or perversion of its intention it has come to be considered as an alien authority.

I shall try to clear up the misunderstanding by making two remarks:

(1) The greater part of the animosity felt by artists and art-lovers against Æsthetics, is, I believe, in reality directed, *not* against Æsthetics, but against *art-criticism*. But Æsthetics and Criticism should not be confused. However closely connected, they are not identical. Yet the intimate connection between them makes the distinction difficult. The difference is primarily a difference in standpoint: the standpoint of Æsthetics is general, that of Criticism is particular; the purpose of Æsthetics is purely cognitive, that of Criticism is discriminating and critical or appreciative; Æsthetics is abstract and theoretical, Criticism is essentially practical. To give an instance: I find myself before some work of Art, a picture, statue, piece of music, dramatic performance or whatever it may be. What interests me in it from the critical point of view? I should like to know whether it pleases me, why it pleases me, why it should please me, whether it pleases everybody, how far my pleasure is representative of the pleasure of the majority of people, what artistic value the work possesses, what claim it may have to lasting fame. Criticism is not, as some people imagine, mainly concerned with finding faults, but also with such *positive* points as those just mentioned. Still all these questions are *critical*. Æsthetics from its general, theoretical, cognitive point of view, is *not* concerned with the appreciation, the good or bad qualities of this particular picture. Æsthetics does not criticise; it only wishes to understand—not so much the concrete production—as the experiences connected with it, the manner of its effect, the mental, emotional, technical labour of its production, the expression of the artist's ideals embodied in it. And it is not interested in these experiences for their own sake, *as* individual experiences, but merely as concrete and representative instances of the kind of experiences usually connected with paintings. Æsthetics, therefore, from *its* standpoint, takes no account either of individual works of Art, or individual appreciation, except as examples or illustrations of the wider problems of artistic production *generally*

E

or æsthetic impression *generally*. To deal with these facts or phenomena *individually*, practically, critically is Criticism, or, if I may
use the expression, 'applied Æsthetics'.

I may, perhaps, make the distinction between Æsthetics and
Criticism clearer by a parallel from another study, that of the
human organism. This analogy, if not pressed too far, will, I think,
explain the point in more than one respect. The relation between
Physiology and Medicine is very similar to that between Æsthetics
and Criticism. Physiology, concerned from its theoretical standpoint with the study of the functions of the human organism, is
not primarily interested in the soundness or unsoundness of the
particular organism it happens to examine. It is not even interested
in this organism *as* an individual organism, be it healthy or
diseased, but only as an illustrative instance of the human organism
in general. An unsound or degenerate organ may even be superior
in demonstrative value for Physiology than a healthy, normal one,
much as curious artistic aberrations are often able to cast more
light upon certain obscure æsthetic problems than a perfect work
of art. Medicine, on the other hand, occupies the practical as distinct from the theoretical, cognitive standpoint. Its object is the
prevention and cure of disease. The abstract interest of Physiology
in the functions of the human body is foreign to it, except as a help
in its practical pursuit. It concerns itself essentially with the *individual*, with the standpoint of soundness reached by the individual, and the concrete causes of the defects or breakdowns of his
physiological machinery. To this extent Medicine might be called
'applied Physiology', namely Physiology applied to the practical
end of the prevention and cure of disease. Physiology, if it interests itself in the question of the normality or abnormality of a
certain organ of a certain individual, abandons its pure physiological standpoint and becomes Medicine or applied Physiology.
It remains pure Physiology only as long as it takes no note of the
individual except as a representative instance. Similarly Æsthetics
disregards individual works of art, except in this special sense.

It is easy to see how the identification of Æsthetics and Criticism has come about. For we must remember that the practical need for criticism preceded chronologically the theoretical conception of æsthetic investigation, just as the practical necessity of curing disease came before, and prepared the way for, physiological research. Thus the applied forms of these studies were the precursors of their pure counterparts, a common state of affairs observable, too, in the relation of Astrology to Astronomy, or of Alchemy to modern Chemistry, or of Occultism to Physical science.[1] And as Medicine is necessarily dependent upon Physiological knowledge and research, so the connection between Criticism and Æsthetics is of the most vital kind. It is true that Criticism often looks disdainfully upon Æsthetics and would fain deny the relationship. Yet it cannot but betray in some measure its æsthetic foundations. Whether superficial or pedantically scholastic, rich in thought or simply intuitive, 'the experiences of a soul among great masters', it is bound to reflect the general æsthetic conceptions, the theory of Art, held by its author, in much the same way as the Chinese expedient of running a red-hot pin through the patient as a cure for intestinal troubles of all description indicates a conception of the human organism different from that of European surgeons. And yet the difference between Æsthetics and Criticism persists. To make the former responsible for all the innumerable imbecilities of the latter is as unwarranted as to charge Physiology with all the medical blunders committed in the pursuit of the practical aim of restoring patients to health.

But our analogy is capable of still further application; it may serve to throw light on the really troublesome question of the æsthetic distinction between 'good' and 'bad' taste. Though not practically concerned in the distinction of healthy or unsound functions of human organs, Physiology is nevertheless capable, within its own sphere and upon its own premises, of establishing this distinction, of offering a criterion of health and disease. According to whether an organ performs its functions in what has

[1] It is of course not my intention to insinuate thereby that Medicine or Criticism stand on the same plane as Astrology, Alchemy or Occultism.

come to be recognised as a normal way, Physiology forms a conception of health or soundness. But it must be noted that it is only the *abstract*, general conception of normality which is purely physiological, not the critical decision of whether this or that special individual organ is healthy or diseased. In the same way, Æsthetics, within its own sphere of theoretical cognition and upon its own premises, distinguishes 'good' from 'bad' taste. This is not Criticism in the usual sense of the word, for Æsthetics is not interested in individual cases of good or bad taste as manifested in response to individual works of art. Naturally the fullest, the most perfect, most subtly differentiated forms of art-impression constitute an æsthetic ideal, i.e. ideally 'good' taste, even as a less perfect, less refined, less richly-woven effect represents a falling off from this ideal, or a less good taste. Even the most rabid opponent of Æsthetics would, I surmise, concede this much as a perfectly justifiable claim. And Æsthetics itself, however much it may elaborate this conception and try to make it more precise, would not go beyond any such general attitude or abandon the theoretical standpoint for a judgment on individual cases or concrete contents. For to abandon its abstract, cognitive position, would be to stop being pure Æsthetics and become applied Æsthetics, i.e. Criticism of individual effects, individual tastes, and individual works.

(2) The second of my remarks has to do with so-called 'rules' in Art.

There are certain rules, or laws, which at various times in the history of Art have been laid down and more or less carefully followed, the observance of which has not infrequently been made the critical standard of a work's excellence. Thus we speak of the law of perspective, the rules of composition, the law of the three Unities, the canons of the human form and a number of others. If it is not the distinction of good and bad taste which excites hostility against Æsthetics, it is, I believe, often the existence of such rules. I therefore ask: what is the attitude of Æsthetics towards rules of this kind and what importance does it attach to them?

It is firstly to be noticed that these rules are not absolute. They merely embody a certain empirically acquired knowledge and are primarily intended to facilitate the execution of work from the artist's point of view. They are precepts, not principles. They are supposed, on the one hand, to assist the artist in the realisation of his ideas and the practice of his art, and, on the other, to assure the maximum of success in the effect of the work. This is evident in a law such as that of perspective. Unfortunately their importance was soon exaggerated. From their purely useful plane they were raised at different times to the status of 'principles of Beauty'. Instead of being regarded as a merely external help to production, they were believed to embody the essence of the Beautiful itself; and inasmuch as a work adhering to them was, *ceteris paribus*, more successful than a work disregarding them, they were made laws of Beauty, critical standards, matters of connoisseurship, all the more welcome as they are easily apprehended and easily verified. For instance, a normal human figure is more likely, under ordinary circumstances, to be beautiful than a hump-backed, crooked or otherwise disfigured body. Hence it was easy to take the step of saying that normality = beauty. A human figure need only be measured to be shown to conform to some canon, Polyclitus', Lysippus', or some other, modern canon, and therefore to be beautiful. The same procedure was adopted for other kinds of artistic objects: certain objective features, characteristics, conditions were deduced from acknowledgedly perfect specimens, proclaimed as principles of Beauty and established as æsthetic laws and critical rules. The flowering period of this process was the time of French classicism, when the 'règles' were paramount and unimpugnable. The war of Romanticism against Classicism, the so-called 'querelle des anciens et des modernes', was mainly waged on these issues. It is hardly necessary to state that modern Æsthetics begs leave to differ from older criticism in this matter of rules and canons.[1]

---

[1] Amusing and instructive instances of the worship of rules abound in that period. In a painstaking work in three vols. by N. Lemercier entitled *Cours analytique de Littérature* (Paris, 1817, vol. I, pp. 177–9), I find a list of twenty-

It is secondly to be noticed that all these 'rules' are not of equal value or intrinsic importance. They might be roughly classed as traditional and technical or material rules. Some of them, the first, have nothing but the glamour of antiquity or the greatness of antique art to support them. Such rules are represented, for instance, by the division of a play into five acts or by the three Unities. Both were at one time considered the *conditio sine qua non* of any good dramatic work of serious pretensions. Their authority rested purely on tradition or on misinterpreted Aristotelian passages, and we nowadays know that as perfect a tragedy can be written in ten or three acts as in five, and in complete disregard of the unity of time and place. A similar rule held that in a painting light and shade should be in approximately equal proportions, and Sir Joshua Reynolds laid it down as a law that pictures ought to be painted predominantly in warm colours. Rembrandt generally reserves only one-eighth of the whole picture for light, and Gainsborough's 'Blue Boy' was the practical rejoinder to Reynolds' assertion. Similarly certain harmonic sequences were at one time regarded as quite inadmissible; until Beethoven and Chopin, Wagner and Brahms proved the unessential and external nature of such 'laws'.

Technical or material rules (sometimes it is feasible, sometimes impossible to make a distinction between these two kinds) are, on the other hand, much less subject to fluctuations. Their authority is not any externally imposed model or generally recognised pattern; it grows out of the requirements of the particular material, manner of handling or consciously proposed effect. In so far they are unimpugnable; until a higher technical development, a refinement of instruments or material makes it possible to discard and supersede them, or a mightier genius can enforce his will in

---

five règles laid down for tragedy alone. Another characteristic example is the following argument from L. B. Castel (*L'Optique des Couleurs*, Paris, 1740): 'La Perspective a ses règles géometriques, le coloris et le clair-obscur sont sans règles; aussi voit-on plus de scavans dessinateurs que de gracieux coloristes: et les Apelles, les Raphaëls sont supérieurs aux Zeuxis et aux Titiens.'

wrestling effects hitherto undreamt of from a refractory or insufficient medium. Thus the technique of fresco-painting is not wholly transferable to oil-painting, or the technique of marble-sculpture to bronze. It was a rule for Greek marble-reliefs that the figures should not project beyond the original surface of the slab or block. This was primarily a question of technique: the Greek sculptor started at once cutting into the marble, leaving the original surface as the nearest parts of his figures; and as nothing could be added to the marble, the highest points of the relief of necessity coincided with the original surface. But when in the Renaissance it became customary, instead of working straight upon the marble from a design or small model, to make first a full-sized clay-model, which was built up from the background instead of being hewn out towards it from the foreground, marble reliefs copied from these models show a very marked projection beyond the apparently original surface. In reality they have no original surface, but appear like the clay-models built up from the background. This is a case of a technical rule upset by modifications of technique. But even the Greeks disregarded the rule when working in metal, in bronze, silver, or gold reliefs, since in these the figures were beaten out of the metal-sheet from behind, and only finished from the front. Here the difference of material, entailing a difference of technical treatment, modifies the rule. From the æsthetic point of view, as I hope to show later on, the difference is not unimportant. But Æsthetics does not make this the ground for any 'rule'.

Lastly, it is another rule (to keep to reliefs) that certain perspective foreshortenings should be avoided because, by their position, they cast shadows upon the background and the other figures, which are liable to distort the whole aspect. This is a rule less externally technical than the preceding one, since it refers to the peculiarities of this whole branch of art rather than to the special requirements of a particular material or its handling. And such rules are of all the least exposed to modifications or changes. At the same time they are the widest and most elastic of all rules.

My purpose in briefly discussing these differences in the value of
'rules' was to emphasise the fact that Æsthetics does not blindly
accept all rules. On the contrary; far from identifying itself with
them, it places itself above them, sifting them and estimating their
scope. It must be clearly understood that these rules are not
*æsthetic*; they are practical, not theoretical; they are precepts, not
principles. Æsthetics is naturally interested in them because of their
connection with the practice of Art. But it takes cognisance of
them merely as facts falling within its sphere of interest, as part of
art-technique in general, or (in the case of traditional rules) as facts
of the History of Art.

The general results of this long discussion of the third popular
objection, might be shortly summarised as follows:

(1) Æsthetics is not to be confounded with Art-Criticism.
(2) The distinction which Æsthetics does make between
    'good' and 'bad' taste is general, abstract, and theoretical,
    not concretely applied to individual cases.
(3) The distinction, even in its general form, is not dogmatic
    or supported by any 'alien' authority.
(4) 'Art-rules' are not laid down by Æsthetics. It merely
    treats them as 'facts' and estimates them as such.

To II. 1. The next objection need not detain us long, although
it opens up problems of a particularly interesting nature. The
argument, if you remember, was from the acknowledged subjectivity of art-impressions to the impossibility of a theoretical and
scientific study of them or of Art in general. The confusion of
ideas and the gap in the argumentation are very obvious: subjectivity is equated with unreality. It is a scientific superstition
(against which Psychology too has had to contend) that only
objects of 'outside reality', things that can be seen, heard, smelt,
felt, weighed, measured, and chemically analysed are 'real'. To
most people there is something derogatory about subjectivity. Yet
this is, as I said, a materialistic prejudice. Purely subjective experience, such as fear or anger, hallucination or dream-image, are

to me, while I have these experiences, as real as any object of 'outside-reality'. More than that; they are much more real than anything else, since they are the only phenomena of which I have first-hand evidence. Everything else I become aware of through the medium of my senses; everything else requires the corroboration of other senses, or of other observers, and frequent verification to assure me of its reality. But of the facts of my subjective experiences no such evidence is needed. I am convinced of their reality by their very existence and by my experience of them.

This may be admitted, and yet the second part of the objection upheld. The experiences of a play, it was said, are unreal, not only because they are subjective, but because the play itself is unreal, an illusion. If I assert that the sympathy which I feel for the tragic hero, the thrills and anxiety at the vicissitudes of his fate are *real* in the sense of the reality of dream-images, *as* subjective experiences, the rejoinder naturally is: but you know perfectly well that it is *only* a play; that the hero who is driven to despair and kills himself, is *only* an actor who is neither really in despair, nor does he really kill himself. Yes; but what does it mean to say that it is *only* a play? Why should it be less 'real', because it is a play? It is of course true that the reality of the play is not the same as that of ordinary common, everyday reality. But this is only because it is not continuous with our ordinary existence.[1] For this same reason we commonly deny 'reality' to our dreams. For this same reason, strange or unusual events of actual, concrete experience often seem to lose their 'reality' and assume the 'unreality' of dreams, if we have no means of bringing them, be it only artificially, into con-

[1] Cf. F. C. S. Schiller, *Studies in Humanism*, 1907, p. 479 f.: 'It may be pointed out that the unreality we allege against ordinary dreams rests really on their intrinsic shortcomings. "Real" and "unreal" are really distinctions of value *within experience*; the "unreal" is what may safely be ignored, the "real" what it is better to recognise. If in our sleep we habitually "dreamt" a coherent experience from night to night, such a dream-life would soon become a "real" life, of which account would be taken, and to which, as in Bulwer Lytton's story, waking life might even be sacrificed. We should have to regard ourselves as living in *two* worlds, and which of them was more "real" would depend largely on the interest we took in our several careers.'

nection with our everyday existence. We can even succeed in deliberately imparting to such actual events the unreality of dreams, by carefully isolating them and suppressing all traces or effects which might constitute such a connection. Thus 'reality' or 'unreality' are simply subjective standpoints or mental attitudes, which we retrospectively occupy or assume. But during the actual experiencing all events, however dream-like they may appear in memory, are real. So, too, the 'illusion' of a play, while it lasts, is not illusory, but real, though real in this special sense, as any event, produced under whatever conditions, but not continuous with our ordinary existence, is real. In order to have a definite term for the kind of reality met with in æsthetic objects, æstheticians have given it the name of 'æsthetic reality'. A discussion of this phenomenon I must reserve for a later occasion.

This objection is, as I said, exceedingly suggestive, and opens up in connection with the question of 'æsthetic reality' a number of problems, such as that of 'æsthetic illusion', which had such a vogue in the eighteenth century and still has even at the present day; the problem of the genuineness or imaginative nature of the emotions both in the artist and the spectator (which was already implied in Aristotle's *Poetics*, and was formally propounded in Didèrot's famous *Dialogue*, 'Le paradoxe sur le Comédien'); and the much-abused theory of the deceptiveness of Art, which was prevalent in the fifteenth and sixteenth centuries, and led to the most weird and absurd conclusions and art 'rules'. To these points I hope to return.

Here I only wish to touch lightly upon the misconception which seems to me the cause of so much sterile wrangling about the reality or unreality of Art.

The fundamental error seems to me to lie in a mistaken co-ordination of reality (in the sense of outside reality) and Art as contradictory opposites, or worse still, in the subordination of the latter to the former as an artificial copy of reality. Modern painting and modern staging with its excessive striving for 'realism', the modern 'naturalistic' novel, all tend to impress upon us this mistaken subordination: the conception of Art as a rendering of persons, states, conditions, characters of an ordinary environment, in short, as a conscious reproduction of reality. Nothing is then more natural than that we should be driven to a comparison unfavourable to Art, since such a reproduction or imitation of reality is bound to fall short, as every copy necessarily falls short, of its original in point of realism. Yet the comparison is inevitable, if these two terms are conceived as antithetically co-ordinate or the one as subordinate to the other: as fiction and reality, or copy and original, or imitation and the thing imitated. It was precisely this correlation which led to the famous theory of art as an 'Imitation of Nature', with all its strange excesses. If Art were merely an imitation of Nature, why are there art-effects in no way corresponding to nature-effects in spite of perfect identity of content? Why have Art at all? There is no use or need for it, since reality we have always with us. Why are there Arts which are obviously not an imitation of Nature at all? The theory places the whole matter on a wrong footing.

There is no need for any such correlation. And if it were not for painting, sculpture, and certain forms of Literature such as the novel and the drama, I doubt whether anyone would ever have hit upon it. Reality and Art are quite well conceivable as two distinct worlds, co-ordinate, if you like, but not correlated, still less the one subordinate to the other. As two distinct spheres they are incommensurable in point of realism, lacking, so to speak, the common denominator for the purpose. Art and reality are at bottom, in spite of superficial resemblances, incomparable, and the whole argument against the reality of Art is fundamentally erroneous, since it starts with this mistaken comparison between Art as a copy and reality as its original. The apparent point of contact between the two spheres is, of course, the rendering in Art of certain objects of reality, notably the human figure in the arts just mentioned, particularly in drama. But this contact, it should be noted, is not genuine. It is something in the nature of an accident, though of an unavoidable accident. For Art is driven, to some extent, to use for its purposes forms of reality, because it cannot in all cases find any other. But, even when it does use them, it uses them only for its own ends, *not as* objects of reality. It does not propose to itself the rendering of real things as its aim. Here is one of the distinctions between painting and photography. Furthermore, the exceptions to this use betray its accidental nature. For there are art-forms which do not belong to objective reality, geometrical patterns and colour-combinations, for example, which are independent of natural originals. Above all there are the forms of that privileged Art, Music. Now, is there any sense in asking whether Music is real or unreal? How could we decide, since we have no point of comparison, no standard whatever, whereby to measure its degree of reality? What is clearly perceptible in the case of Music, is also true of the other arts, though in them the state of affairs may be more or less obscured by the inevitable necessity of using the forms of reality. Whither such a comparison can logically lead via the 'Imitation Theory', is comically illustrated by the views of two Renaissance critics as to what Aristotle may have meant by 'a single revolution of the sun', to which, as he said, the action of Greek drama was generally confined. The one, Robortelli, pleaded for the artificial day of twelve hours, since, he said, the action ought to be continuous, and people were accustomed to sleep at night. Segni, his opponent, was of opinion that twenty-four hours must be meant, because, since murders, adulteries, and other dreadful and tragic deeds were usually done at night, the action of the tragedy ought also, for the sake of greater realism, to comprise the time from 6 p.m. to 6 a.m. To Robortelli's argument that it was contrary to Nature, not to sleep at night, Segni answers that nothing would be more natural for villainous and unjust people such as tragic characters than to act contrary to the laws of Nature.[1]

---

[1] See for the dispute: J. E. Spingarn, *Literary Criticism in the Renaissance*, New York, 1899, p. 92.

This sounds like a joke; but Robortelli seems in deadly earnest. Here is the text: 'Verba Graeca sunt μίαν περίοδον ἡλίου quae etsi ambigua videri possunt; significent ne diem naturalem a mathematicis astronomis vulgo vocatum an artificialem: putarim tamen ego ab Aristotele intellegi arti-

To II. 2. Still shorter can be the rejoinder to the objection which asserts that the non-intellectual, or at least not wholly intellectual, nature of æsthetic experiences renders it impossible to account for them in purely intellectual terms. The passage from the review I quoted is a singular instance of such a misconception. The author boldly condemns all Æsthetics as futile, although he does not seem to know what the Æsthetics of the present time is really aiming at. To quote Tolstoy's book as representative of this modern conception is unfair both to Tolstoy and to modern Æsthetics. The reviewer begins by stating that 'a definition of Beauty is an attempt to understand beauty by means of the intellect alone' (the idea that the end of Æsthetics is to give a definition of Beauty is a widespread superstition, but let that pass at present); 'but since', he goes on to say, 'our experience of beautiful things is not purely intellectual, we cannot express that experience in purely intellectual terms'. This is very interesting. It sounds as if the author meant to imply that only purely intellectual experiences are expressible in intellectual terms. Has it occurred to him that by this argument he disproves not only Æsthetics but a great many other Sciences? If I say that the sum of the angles of a triangle is equal to two right angles, I suppose that I intellectually express a fact. But is this fact purely intellectual? If I see the moon turning round the earth, or if an apple falls from a tree, or even if I myself fell from a tree, which does not seem to be a purely intellectual experience, surely I can, in a sense, express this experience, even in the most intellectual terms, in a mathematical formula. One wonders what the author means by 'expressing an experience'? What he means by 'expressing it in terms of pure reason'? For the purposes of Æsthetics it is quite sufficient, if 'expressing' means 'to render an account of' or 'to account for' an experience. It does not,

---

ficialem ... maxime aequum est, ut actionis imitatio sit, quae uno die videatur absoluta; noctu enim homines conquiescunt indulgentque somno; necque quidpiam agunt, aut ulla de re inter se colloquuntur.' (Robortelli, *In librum Aristotelis de arte poetica explicationes*, Florentiae, 1548, p. 50.) I have unfortunately not seen the text of Segni.

of course, mean *to have the experience itself*. Yet this is what he seems to imply, when he continues: 'No amount of hard thinking will enable a man to know a good picture from a bad one.' No doubt, this is very true; but Æsthetics does not assume that to think about a picture is equivalent to having an æsthetic experience of that picture. On the contrary, Æsthetics would call that a *non*-æsthetic experience. But when I have had the æsthetic experience, I presume that I can think about, not only the picture, but my experience of it. It is the same with other common experiences, which imply 'the use of all my faculties'. Thus, if I feel angry, seeing someone ill-treat an animal, for instance, I have an experience which is partly intellectual, to some extent sensational and volitional, but predominantly emotional. Why should I not be able to account for it? Granted, no amount of hard thinking will make me realise what I *felt* like, while I *was* angry; that can only be realised while the experience lasts, i.e. while I am angry. But surely I can account for it intellectually after the experience. I can rationally explain why I was angry and why this particular act of brutality made me angry. So in the case of a picture; it is no use just *thinking about* the picture; I must have experienced it 'by the use of all my faculties'. But then I can think as hard as I like about the experience in reference to the picture and indicate the causes of my experience, its general character, its development, its defects and its virtues. Modern Æsthetics does not want to think about the picture, but primarily about the experience of it. This is the principal misconception in the passage. Compared with this, it is relatively unimportant that the author also confuses Æsthetics and Art-Criticism, one of the leading defects of the book he was reviewing. For Æsthetics, as I pointed out before, is not interested in distinguishing a certain good picture from a certain bad one; it is not even interested in the special experience of a special individual before this certain good or bad picture. One of its subjects is æsthetic experience in general as produced, for instance, by painting in general. But this matter has already been discussed and I turn, therefore, to the last objection.

To II. 3. This objection I quoted in the words of Walter Pater. It asserted the impossibility and uselessness of formulating abstract definitions of Beauty, since 'such discussions help us very little to enjoy what has been well-done in art or poetry, to discriminate between what is more and what is less excellent in them, or to use words like beauty, excellence, art, poetry, with a more precise meaning than they would otherwise have. Beauty like most other qualities presented to the human mind is relative; and a definition becomes meaningless and useless in proportion to its abstractness.'

I must state at once that this objection is in my eyes no objection at all, at least not to Æsthetics in its modern form. On the contrary, I most cordially agree with Pater. It must only be pointed out that present Æsthetics is in no way hit by the argument, since, as I have just said, its object is not to formulate definitions of Beauty. What in the previous writer is a regrettable lack of acquaintanceship with modern developments in Æsthetics is, in the case of Pater, cause for admiration. For these words were not written, as were the others in 1907, but in the sixties of the last century, at a time when Æsthetics still strove strenuously to complete the Sisyphus-labour of a definition of Beauty, and therein pursued an ambition which we cannot at the present day but consider sterile, if not definitely misleading and false. I cannot help feeling that if Pater could have foreseen the new standpoint, and if he had realised how much more liberal and comprehensive the whole conception of Æsthetics has become, he would have felt more sympathy with it and shown greater appreciation of the services which it may in its own way render to a fuller comprehension of Art. He would also have realised the distinction between Æsthetics and Criticism of which, as the passage shows, he was unaware: the one setting out for the understanding of aesthetic experiences and the aesthetic consciousness as science sets out for understanding of the objective phenomena which it studies—the other helping to deepen individual experiences themselves, evoking them in all their wealth in duller and less appreciative minds and endeavouring to give them their most adequate, complete, and concrete expression. This is an art in itself, requiring unlimited enthusiasm and infinite love of Art in all its forms.

To the illustration of this wider conception of Æsthetics I now proceed.

## II

The last point discussed may serve as a transition to the positive, in distinction to the preceding negative, circumscription of the field. If before I tried to show (with the assistance of various arguments which all impute to it some objectionable or impossible intention or purpose) what Æsthetics is *not*, and what it does *not* propose to itself as an end, I now wish to explain, what it is, what its purpose, its function and its range have come to be at the present day. It will be seen that its scope has gradually widened and occupied, one after another, fields of investigation, which were previously considered non-existent, or were neglected either as unimportant or as being outside the scope of the subject. Æsthetics in this respect reminds one of the ripples on the water caused by a stone dropped into it. The many endeavours to arrive at some kind of definition, which should once and for all tell us what Beauty is, represent the first contact of the stone with the surface of the water. And since the first stone was dropped in, innumerable others have been thrown after it, without, however, producing ripples strong enough to propagate themselves over the whole of the lake. The opposition of Pater to such definitions is, as I said, all the more remarkable, since at that time it was still the custom to drop stones into the water, i.e. to make logical definitions. I should not stress this point if it were not still a widespread popular superstition that it is the special business of Æsthetics to provide a definition of Beauty. If this is a reason for some people to reject it, it is also a reason for others to look up to it, rather eagerly and expectantly, as a form of speculation, which might place into everyone's hands, in the shape of a definition, the means of distinguishing infallibly the Beautiful from the Ugly. Our manner of speaking would, if nothing else, lead us to believe that

Beauty is either a thing or a quality, which need only be defined or described to be recognised and identified as such in any object commonly admitted to be beautiful. Much in the same way as Chemistry demonstrates by analysis the presence of oxygen in something, whereupon the thing is said to contain oxygen, so Æsthetics is expected to demonstrate the presence of Beauty in a work of art, whereupon the work is said to be beautiful.

In this bald formulation, the notion may appear exaggeratedly childish, but I believe that something of this kind is really the task popularly assigned to Æsthetics. And this conception has in various forms actually been the road from which for centuries æsthetic problems have been approached.[1] Most æsthetic speculation of preceding ages can be brought under three heads:

(1) The problem of a *definition of Beauty* in terms of an idea.
(2) The problem of a *criterion of Beauty*.
(3) The problem of a *cause of Beauty*.

The first tries to solve the question: What is Beauty? the second asks: How do I know, whether a thing is beautiful? and the third: What causes a thing to be beautiful?

(1) Under the first head would fall all the various definitions which identified Beauty with utility (Socrates), with knowledge (Plato and, in a different form, Baumgarten and the whole rationalistic school of thought), with a deity (Plotinus and many other subsequent metaphysical æstheticians), with perfection, with the ethically good, etc., not to speak of those purely metaphysical views which explain Beauty as the Infinite revealed in the Finite, or as the manifestation of the Idea in concrete form. To enter upon a discussion of these problems and a criticism of such definitions is not my intention. This belongs rather to the History of Æsthetics. The point which cannot fail to strike the unsophisticated mind is that some of these statements may be true in a sense, but only true

---

[1] In the following remarks I am greatly indebted to E. Kulke, *Kritik der Philosophie des Schönen*, Leipzig, 1906, where a full development of the arguments against these kinds of theories will be found.

F

in the general abstract form of the definition, meaningless if applied to concrete cases. Some of them, besides, form part of, and are conditioned in their sense and application by, definite metaphysical systems, so that only our approval of the system can extort our consent to its definition of Beauty. If we are told that Beauty is knowledge, or perfection, we stand amazed and vaguely murmur: Possibly, but what does that mean? And the less we are philosophers and the more we are artists or fond of art, the more do we feel inclined to agree that 'to define Beauty not in the most abstract, but in the most concrete terms possible . . . is the aim of the true student of Æsthetics'.

(2) The problem of the *criterion of Beauty* appeals with infinitely more force to our desire to understand the mystery of the Beautiful. We have only to run through the index of Burke's Treatise on the *Sublime and the Beautiful* to find a whole catalogue of features enumerated, which are supposed to represent such criteria. Smallness, smoothness, gradual variation in contour or surface, delicacy, gracefulness, brightness and purity of colour are the characteristics of beautiful objects which he mentions, and each one separately or in conjunction with others is to constitute the criterion of Beauty. At the same time, everyone must, on the least consideration, realise how profoundly unsatisfactory this whole notion of enumerating certain objective qualities as criteria of Beauty necessarily is. To the most inexperienced mind scores of things must occur which either flatly contradict the qualities named or are outside their range altogether. In view of this difficulty the criterion of Beauty was also sought not in definite single qualities but in the *manner* in which they are combined or adjusted to each other. In this way we come to theories which set out to discover definite relations of individual parts of a whole to each other or to the whole. Regularity, evenness, symmetry, proportion, measure, harmony, etc., have been declared to be such criteria. But the result has always been the same: there are beautiful objects which either lack these features altogether or but imperfectly conform to them.

(3) This last-named conception has also been offered as a solution to the problem of the *cause* of Beauty. If we ask what makes an object appear beautiful, we are told that a certain ratio or proportion in the relation of its parts to each other is the cause or condition of its Beauty. Thus F. Hutcheson enunciated his law of 'unity in variety' (which, of course, goes back to antiquity), and Zeising quite recently (1854) proclaimed his principle of the 'golden section' (approximately 3:5) as the fundamental cause of all Beauty. This idea received a powerful impetus from certain scientific discoveries: the discovery that two harmonious or consonant notes stand to each other in definite simple ratios; Helmholtz's discovery of the ratios of overtones conditioning harmonies and dissonances and similar facts which have been sought and, as many believe, verified in respect of colours and colour-combinations; the apparent confirmation of such theories by archæological discoveries and the measurements of ancient buildings, temples and statues. The simplicity, and the apparent scientific precision, of the theory have something seductive about them, in spite of the fact that its abstractness and rigidity make it repellent to imaginative minds. However this may be, the main obstacle to its acceptance lies elsewhere. If you or I or 'the man in the street' constructed ever so many figures, or statues, or houses, or patterns upon the golden section or any other accredited proportion, would they be beautiful? I doubt it very much. Yet they ought to be, since the 'cause of Beauty', the proportion is there. How is this? I make no doubt Michelangelo would have drawn a figure or shaped a statue without first constructing its skeleton upon the golden section, and it would have been beautiful, whether the golden section were there or not. The theory unfortunately makes no allowance for genius. And secondly, if the principle held good, nothing ought to be easier than to demonstrate Beauty, as you demonstrate geometrically that two sides of a triangle are longer than the third. Nobody in his right mind can refuse to be convinced of this. But the lack of consensus in æsthetic matters is also an undoubted fact and with the acknowledgment of this, all theories propounding

objective causes of Beauty must inevitably break down. For
Beauty is *not* logically demonstrable, as it ought to be if it had an
objective cause. It is precisely to these kinds of æsthetic theories
that the lack of consensus of opinion, often urged as an objection
to Æsthetics in general, is absolutely fatal.

All theories which approach the problems of Æsthetics by any
of these three roads have two common features in their methods,
and it is the assumptions underlying these features which make the
theories so unbending and so unconformable to concrete experiences. The first is the belief in the objectivity of Beauty. And the
other, causally connected with it in many cases, is the conviction
that Beauty in general, the 'absolutely Beautiful', is a whole and
indivisible entity existing somehow independently of beautiful
things, much as the Platonic 'idea' exists independently of its concrete manifestation. Thus to identify Beauty with knowledge, or
with perfection, is an attempt to define this 'absolutely Beautiful'
in terms of an idea, which may be, so to speak, incarnated in
various objects of Beauty as individual or concrete forms of knowledge or perfection. Burke's catalogue of objective qualities of
Beauty is arrived at by deducing qualities from different particular
objects of beauty. Generalised and combined, they are then said to
be features of the 'absolute Beauty'. The impossibility of charac-
terising something absolute in terms of such qualities as smallness,
smoothness, etc., is evident. The theories relying on proportion,
harmony, unity-in-variety, etc., are an endeavour to empty the
definition still further of individual content, to render it as general
and abstract as possible, in the hope of arriving at some formulation of that which *ex hypothesi* possesses no concrete content. And
this conception of Beauty has been reflected back upon the notion
of Art. Art, in general, is then thought to be the concrete manifestation of this purely abstract and empty thing, Beauty. Inasmuch as, for instance, the golden section is found in an individual
painting or statue, that painting or that statue is said to be a
particular form or expression of that general 'absolute Beauty',
namely the ratio 3:5.

If we check this against actual experience, the failure of such theories as well as the cause of their barrenness becomes evident at once. The idea of an absolute Beauty above or apart from its special manifestations in works of art seems, in the light of our experience of beautiful things, something entirely empty, and also impossible, since we cannot form any conception of Beauty apart from some actual concrete thing which is or appears beautiful. Yet this abandoning of the idea of absolute Beauty as the special objective of Æsthetics is an insight which is only the outcome of recent thought. There is no absolute Beauty, neither as an abstract idea nor as a universal objective quality, which might be in greater or lesser degree concreted or incarnated in Art.[1] This conviction has been growing out of speculations on Art rather than on Beauty;

---

[1] The point is to recognise '*absolute Beauty*' for what it really is: a purely *verbal abstraction*. The difficulty is that everyone believes in it, though few attribute to it a higher kind of reality, as metaphysicians are wont to do. What the majority of people mean, when they say that they believe in 'absolute Beauty', is an ideal abstracted from the totality of their several, individual experiences of *concrete* Beauty. But this does not make it into an actually existing entity of superior reality. On the contrary. This 'absolute Beauty', as expression of the totality of an individual experience, remains necessarily individually limited and conditioned by the character of such individual experiences. As such it is discussable and explicable, as most of our 'general ideas' are, namely explicable in reference to its origin and development.

*De jure* all such 'absolute Beauties' have an equal right to existence—but *de facto* we recognise superior and inferior notions of 'absolute Beauty'. The reason for the attribution of superiority to some lies in the *intrinsic value* of the particular conception. The intrinsic value of a conception of Beauty resides in its superior capacity to cover *all* æsthetic experiences: The wider, the more comprehensive, the subtler the conception is, the higher its intrinsic value, and *he* has the better right to impose *his* idea of Beauty as the superior notion, who has the finest feeling for the Beautiful within his experience; who enjoys most, feels deepest, and possesses the widest field of æsthetic pleasure. Not the most *eclectic* and fastidious taste, but the most *catholic* taste has the claim to superiority.

Thus 'absolute Beauty' is not an *a priori* conception of superior validity, or a standard whereby to measure æsthetic experiences, but rather an *ex-post-facto* interpretation of past individual experiences, i.e. a conception which has nothing 'absolute' about it, but which is continually being formed, enlarged, subtilised, rectified and verified.

and it is the correlate to the belief that there is strictly speaking no Art any more than there is Science. There are only sciences, and only arts. No doubt we may speak of Art collectively, as a convenient figure of speech, but again in reality and in our actual experience there are only the individual, differentiated arts. In fact, the higher our appreciation is developed, the subtler our sensitiveness to æsthetic effects becomes, the less can we admit any identification or even equivalence of any two arts. In other words, Beauty collectively, this same absolute, abstract, indivisible Beauty (even if we could in any way conceive of it) is not something which can at will be translated now into Poetry, now into Painting, now into Statuary, and now into Music. The notion that the beauty of Poetry is the same as, or interchangeable with, the beauty of Statuary is a theoretical crudity which Æsthetics is fortunately on the way to overcoming. There are beautiful statues, beautiful poems and beautiful music, but these various representatives of Art are not beautiful in the same manner: each is beautiful in its own way, and the appreciation of each is the more perfect and the more complete, the more its distinctive and peculiar kind of beauty is felt to be distinct from the beauty of other arts.

But why stop there? If we distinguish between the Beauty of Poetry, Sculpture, Painting, Architecture, Music, etc., why not go further? In fact, the differentiations extend far beyond the divisions of the arts. Even *within* the same art we cannot reasonably maintain that the beauty of a marble statue is the same as that of a bronze; that an oil-painting is beautiful in the same way as a watercolour or a fresco, or a lyrical poem as a novel, or a tragedy as a comedy, or a sonata as an opera. Here again a refined sensibility revolts against the artificiality of theoretically labelling one art as a thoroughly homogeneous group in complete disregard of the peculiarities of its sub-divisions. And more than this: the differences extend even to the individual works of art. The Doryphoros of Polycletus does not offer the same kind of beauty as Michelangelo's David, or a statue by Rodin; or a Madonna of Botticelli the same kind as Holbein's Virgin, although the three former may be marble statues, and the two latter oil-paintings of identical subjects. If we obliterate theoretically the differences between the semi-transparent, finely-granulated surface of the marble with its softness of outline and the polished, hard-cut and sharply-chiselled features of the bronze, or the contrast between the heroic serenity and ease of the Greek sculpture and the concentrated fire and tension of Michelangelo's statue, do we not destroy just that particular beauty which is the special possession and unique charm of each material or each work? In doing so for the sake of æsthetic theory, we not only lose contact with the immediacy and fulness of experience; we falsify the experience itself, simplyfying it and abstracting from it all its content of Beauty, and giving in exchange but empty shells of verbal definitions. Is it any wonder that Æsthetics has made itself ridiculous, when it presumed to exhaust the beauty of the Doryphoros or the David by explaining that in both the body is to the legs as 3 is to 5?

However crude this sounds, this has in substance been at times the highest ambition of Æsthetics, and it is significant that Lessing's *Laokoon*, in which he attempted to establish the limits between poetry and the plastic arts and which at the time of its publication was epoch-making, is practically contemporaneous with Batteux's theory of arts 'réduits à un seul principe'. Both are characteristic of this conception of Æsthetics: the latter aiming at a theory of the 'absolutely Beautiful', the former drawing distinctions childishly obvious to any appreciation which has not been theoretically adulterated.

The Æsthetics of today, far from wishing to reduce Beauty to one principle or to some dialectically formulated definition, is on the contrary anxious to preserve the distinctions and to deepen the differences between the various arts and their effects. If I may venture to put forward a view to which I strongly incline, I may say that any beautiful thing *appears to me absolutely and fundamentally incomparable in point of Beauty to any other beautiful thing, however similar in subject, conception or technique*; that in matters of appreciation there is no superlative, but only an elative; that æsthetic judgments in this sense are never relative, but always absolute, and that comparisons are not only proverbially invidious, but the ruin of all genuine appreciation.

\*     \*     \*

In view of misunderstandings, I will repeat with some supplementary remarks the argument in favour of the thesis, that:

*Things of Beauty are fundamentally incomparable with each other in point of Beauty.*

There is a possible ambiguity in the term '*incomparable*'. 'To compare' can here be taken in two different senses:

1. 'To notice *differences and similarities*', in practice it will principally be a question of noticing *differences*. The fundamental question of comparing 'things of Beauty' in *this* sense is: 'Wherein do things of Beauty differ from each other?'

2. '*To compare in point of value.*' The formulation of the question in this second sense is: 'Is one thing of Beauty more beautiful than another thing of Beauty?'

It is in this second sense that I used the term 'incomparable' in my statement. I tried to make its meaning sufficiently clear by saying: 'Things of Beauty are incomparable with each other *in point of Beauty.*' Note that I speak of *things of Beauty*, meaning things which we actually feel to be beautiful, things which we *appreciate* as beautiful. I am *not* speaking of things which may be beautiful, but which we do *not*, for some reason or other, appreciate as such.

It is for me primarily a QUESTION OF FACT. I wished to establish *a fact of psychological experience*: that we actually feel things of Beauty, things which we appreciate, to be incomparable with each other in point of Beauty.

This is the *main* point. Subsequently there arises a QUESTION OF PRINCIPLE, which is really irrelevant to the argument of these lectures, but is of considerable general interest: namely, the question of *whether comparison has any value in relation to our appreciation of works of art.*

## I. THE QUESTION OF FACT

I tried to narrow down the argument which was to establish the fact of the incomparability of individual works of art, in so far as we actually appreciate them, by stating the following points in succession:

(1) It is evident, if we question our experience, that works belonging to *different* arts cannot in this way (i.e. with regard to their beauty of effect) be compared. This is a most obvious truth. A Sonata and a cathedral, a poem and a statue, a tragedy and a painting are things which differ so radically from each other in character that our impressions do not admit of comparison, since they are so completely unlike each other *in kind*.

In order to prevent fresh misunderstanding, let me say at once, that when I speak of effect, impression, I do *not* mean simply the *pleasure* we derive from a work of art. *Pleasures*, so psychologists tell us, in the strictly psychological sense of the term, differ only in *intensity*, not in *quality*. The ordinary usage of the word 'pleasure' is so lax and indefinite that to use it here would quite unnecessarily complicate the discussion. 'Pleasure', I should say, is a very minor part of the whole æsthetic phenomenon. It is merely the 'epiphenomenon', the tail-end of what I call the impression or effect. *Impressions* differ not only in intensity, but especially in *kind* or *quality*. The impression which a building gives us, is a different thing from the impression we get from a poem or a painting, though the pleasure we get from both may be of equal intensity.

(2) My second step was the point that things belonging to *different sub-divisions* of even the *same* art are equally incommensurable in effect, because here again our impressions differ in kind, as they do with things belonging to different arts. The realisation of these differences in kind is a matter of some æsthetic experience. A person devoid of art-education and training of taste will hardly realise them at all. But with progressing experience and increasing sensitiveness these differences become gradually sharper. The finer and more acute our appreciation becomes, the more intensely we

realise the beauty of one special group (say of *marble* as distinct from *bronze* sculpture), the less can we admit the homogeneity of *sculpture* as one and the same kind of art. Similarly in painting: the undoubted dullness of frescoes compared with the transparency of oils will be realised not as a *defect* of fresco-painting, but merely as a *peculiarity* of it, and, when we have learnt to appreciate frescoes, even as a *virtue*. The man who objects to frescoes, because they are not like oil-paintings, is like a man who complains because an apple does not taste like an orange. He is, of course, as much at liberty to dislike frescoes as to prefer apples to oranges.

*In short*, we can as little compare, in point of beauty, a marble statue with a bronze, a song with a nocturne, or a comedy with a tragedy, as we can compare a statue with a painting or a novel with a vase. In the case of things belonging to different sub-divisions of the same art, the comparison *appears* more feasible. But this is only because we reach the point of feeling that these things actually do differ *in kind* much later on in our æsthetic development and as a result of much greater sensitiveness to art-impressions.

(3) The incomparability, I suggested, might be carried further, beyond the divisions of the arts and the sub-divisions of each separate art, even into the appreciation of *individual works*. In fact I understate the case by saying that 'it *might* be carried into the appreciation of individual works'. I *know* this to be a *fact*.

My point is that any individual work, whenever we actually and fully appreciate it, becomes *ipso facto incomparable in point of beauty* with any other work. For intense appreciation implies *eo ipso* the recognition of its uniqueness, of those distinctive qualities, which are its exclusive property, and make it different from, and incommensurable with, any other work, however similar in subject, conception or technique. The more we appreciate it, the more we let ourselves be imbued with its spirit and enveloped by its peculiar atmosphere, the stronger do we realise its uniqueness and solitary perfection. Conversely, the more we realise a work as an individual entity, distinct from anything else, the more we may be said to appreciate it.

The difficulty of theoretically illustrating the point is this. If I say: Imagine the Doryphoros of Polycletus and Michelangelo's David, by the very selection of *two* individual objects, a comparison is *forced* upon many people. You may never have appreciated either the one or the other. And so it is with other pairs of things. In these psychological matters we must needs speak of ourselves. If I therefore give examples, I do not mean that they must necessarily carry the same weight with you as they do with me. For your own satisfaction you must think of works which you too appreciate: A Madonna of Botticelli: The Sistine Madonna; The Parthenon: Notre Dame; *Fidelio*: *Tannhäuser*; Landscape by Turner: Landscape by Böcklin; The Nike of Paionios: The Nike in the Louvre; Valse by Chopin: Valse by Strauss; *Vanity Fair*: *David Copperfield*; etc., etc. *In short*: my contention is this:

(1) Comparisons of value do *not spontaneously* arise in appreciation; on the contrary, genuine and full appreciation is characterised by the feeling that the thing appreciated is unique and of entirely different complexion from any other work.

(2) The preoccupation of making comparisons of value, forced upon us either by an external authority or by habits of thought, bars our way to full appreciation and is hostile to fully-realised effects.

This is *not* to advocate 'blind enthusiasm' or 'uncritical admiration' (an intention which has been imputed to me). The question of criticism belongs to the point of principle, which I am coming to presently. It is a side-issue of the present discussion, but strictly speaking irrelevant to it. All I wish to maintain for the argument of these lectures is that, in point of fact and as a truth of psychological experience, our appreciation need not and does not involve a conscious comparison of value between the thing we appreciate and any other thing, because appreciation means the recognition of this particular thing as something unique and distinct in kind from any other thing.

It is in this sense that I said: *appreciation is always* ELATIVE, *but not* SUPERLATIVE.

It was in the same sense that I called æsthetic appreciation *absolute*. But it will be remembered that I added, that it is, of course, *relative* to the individual's æsthetic development, to his sensitiveness and his education in art-effects.

In support of this contention I would add that, as people grow older and develop in æsthetic experience, EXCLUSIVE *preferences* for certain works decrease. This is *not*, of course, due to a *weakening* of sensitivity or of critical faculties. It is, on the contrary, the result of enlarged and refined susceptibilities and of wider æsthetic experience. Everyone remembers the time, when, as a boy, he thought that there was no book like Cooper's *Last of the Mohicans* or some similar tale of adventure. But this need for preferences of an exclusive kind, the feeling that one could not possibly appreciate two or more things equally, gradually disappears. The wider one's outlook becomes, the more one comes into intimate contact with great works, the less becomes the desire for rigidly assessing each admired thing in a graduated scale of preferences. And the more sensitive and acute one's appreciation grows, the less able and inclined one feels to abstract from the individual features and unique character of any work of supreme beauty for the mere satisfaction of saying: this I think more beautiful than that. Only then does one realise the invidiousness of such comparisons, the inevitable injustice towards each work that it implies and the impairing of appreciation it involves. Nor is there any need for graduated preferences. The hankering after it is frequently merely a habit of thought. It is true that many people, perhaps constitutionally, cannot rid themselves of it, just as some people may be worried by doubts as to which of their friends they like best.

So far the question of *fact*. Its establishment is of considerable importance to my whole argument on æsthetic phenomena, and I have therefore insisted on it to this extent. If I may with a word anticipate the future development of that argument to explain the importance I attach to this fact, I would say that this 'incomparability' is precisely one of the great characteristics of Beauty. Whenever we find ourselves contemplating anything, be it a living person or a historical character, a landscape, a flower or a work of art, in this manner, appreciating it in its quite peculiar, unique and distinctive individuality which belongs to it alone and to nothing else, and which to our feeling makes it incomparable to anything else—then we appreciate that thing *æsthetically*.

## II. THE QUESTION OF PRINCIPLE

This question might be formulated thus:

'Although appreciation itself involves no conscious comparison between one work and another, is there any sense at all in which comparison might play a part in relation to appreciation?'

I. I am willing to admit:

    a. That there may be evaluation or comparison of the value of one work with that of others, *subsequently* to and *based upon* appreciation;

    b. That there may be a *noticing of differences in detail*, i.e. comparison in the first sense, also *subsequently to* appreciation.

II. But I *protest* against comparison-evaluation *previous to* and *with a view to appreciation*.

Ia. The first point is almost self-evident. Looked at from the outside, appreciation of any work *ipso facto* implies, potentially and ultimately, an evaluation, a distinguishing, an assessment of the value of the work appreciated to the disadvantage of other works, though I may not specify any individual works and may not *consciously* make any such distinction in value. If in a museum I appreciate the Venus of Milo, I do *objectively*, in the eyes perhaps of another person who watches me, make an implicit comparison of value between the Venus of Milo and, say, the Venus de Medici which stands by her side. I may not even have noticed the Venus de Medici. Still the fact remains that my appreciation of the Venus of Milo implies a selection, a choice and, in that sense, an evaluation of her to the disadvantage of the Venus de Medici. It is this fact, very probably, which has given rise to the idea that appreciation must needs imply a comparison *subjectively*. But this is a mistake. There is no contradiction between the admission here and my original statement that appreciation is non-comparative. Although from the outside my appreciation of the Venus of Milo implies a preference for her over the Venus de Medici, my appreciation is not, *subjectively*, based upon any comparison between them.

Ib. With this second point we come to the question of *criticism*.

I must again repudiate most emphatically the suggestion that, because I hold appreciation to be non-comparative, I mean to advocate 'blind enthusiasm' or 'uncritical admiration'. I do wish to advocate admiration and enthusiasm, certainly; but there is no reason why they should be uncritical or blind, though even blind but whole-hearted enthusiasm might be worth more than the flaccid, blasé superciliousness which so often passes for critical sagacity.

Nor is it my intention to attack criticism as a whole, to set up arbitrary standards of individual caprice and further anarchical conditions. Here, as elsewhere, this would mean the predominance of mediocrity. Hence, though I insist that active appreciation is not only not identical with, but even hostile to, the critical attitude, I see no reason why *subsequent* criticism should not find its place in our scheme.

Let us assume that I appreciate a picture. I like it at first sight, I lose myself in its contemplation, it speaks to me of things that I seem intently to listen to, it assumes life before my eyes, it envelops me with its quite peculiar atmosphere—in fact, I 'experience' the painting, realise it æsthetically. Nothing whatever stands in the way of my then trying to account to myself *why* I like, appreciate and admire it. On the contrary, it is most desirable and important that I should attempt rationally to understand my appreciation. Here criticism begins.

But there are various *kinds* of criticism. Criticism which compares details of one work with details of another, *comparative* criticism, is not the *only* kind. I may try to account for my appreciation without consciously adducing any other work for comparison. I may say to myself: How magnificent this piece of colour is, how wonderfully fine this drawing! Look how subtly the artist has wrought the expression of this face! What a fascinating contradiction between those heavy dreamy eyes and the fleeting irony round the lips! I wonder what it is that gives this peculiar reposeful quiet to the whole picture? Is it the colour-harmony, or the balance of light and shade, or the distribution of the masses? Or is it the wide expanse of background with its splendid perspective and its bluish-grey distance?

All these are or imply *critical* questions. By their help I try to understand *why* I should have been affected by this particular picture in this particular way, a way in which no other picture has previously affected me. Yet there is no *comparison*. The proceedure is purely *analytic*, an analysis of this single picture, without looking past it to any other work.

It is, however, quite possible, and sometimes advantageous, to notice differences in details between individual works, to assist analysis and throw into relief the peculiarities of one or both works. But as a corrective to exaggerated attention to minor details, I would recall what an artist friend of mine once said to me: 'Whenever you find that any special point, of technique or rendering or conception, obtrudes itself and tends to monopolise your attention to the detriment of the impression of the whole, you can be sure that there is something wrong with the work.' With this proviso, we may say that a comparison of *details*, whether between works of superior and inferior merit or between two works which you equally appreciate, will certainly *deepen* the distinction between them and thus still more accentuate their uniqueness instead of obscuring and diminishing it as does a comparison of works *in toto*.

By such criticism, which does not find its immediate task in pronouncing whether such and such a work is better or worse than some other work, but which, without any preconceived notions of a scale of merit, 'rationalises' our appreciation, we gain æsthetic experience, develop our taste, and refine our sensitiveness.

The ideal, an ideal actually reached with wide experience, is that not only appreciation, but even criticism should be non-comparative: that the individual should know *intuitively* whether a work is of superior or inferior merit; that his taste should be so sure and refined that he at once detects any falling-off of a work from the best that he is accustomed to, his sensitiveness tuned to such a pitch that he can say directly whether a work rings true or not. This is what I had in mind when I said that appreciation is *absolute*, though relative to the individual's development: a kind of comparison not between *individual* works, but between this work now before him and his own taste, which represents his *cumulative experience* of the best that can be found.

II. For these reasons I renew my protest against *comparisons of value* in so far as they are undertaken *with a view to appreciation*. If I have been rightly understood, it may even be doubted whether it ever happens. Unfortunately it does. Many individuals have a perfect mania for preference-judgments. They cannot rest content unless everything is pigeon-holed in a hierarchy of value. They *dare* not appreciate, unless they have assured themselves that the work is actually worth appreciating. They approach a work with the question 'Does it possess merit? If so, I will like it'. They reverse the actual process of true appreciation which says 'I like it, therefore I appreciate it—*why* do I appreciate it—*wherein does its merit consist?*' Their point of view has even been sanctioned by the astounding theory of Kant—possibly one of the most inartistic persons who have ever speculated upon Art—that æsthetic judgment *precedes* appreciation, that we *judge* a flower to be beautiful and *therefore* like it (the famous synthetic judgment *a priori*).

In another respect, too, many are amazingly narrow-minded, or rather narrow-*hearted*. They cannot appreciate and admire two things at the same time. To them, liking one thing excludes liking another. They feel it a contradiction to admire Mozart *and* Brahms. If they like Greek architecture, they cannot admire Gothic. If they like old Renaissance paintings, they abominate the modern Impressionists. Something of the kind happened (through another form of bias) to even so appreciative a mind as Ruskin's, with its unbounded admiration for Gothic and its equally un-bounded contempt for Renaissance architecture.

It cannot be too strongly emphasised, as a retort to the belief that eclecticism and fastidiousness are æsthetic virtues, that a re-stricted number of preferences is one of the surest signs of æsthetic poverty and impotence. In some cases it merely indicates lack of æsthetic experience. But many people actually pride themselves on liking only a very few, specially selected works. They usually never realise what a fearful *testimonium paupertatis* they thereby give themselves. As I said before,[1] it is not the eclectic and fas-tidious taste which can claim superiority, it is *width of sympathy* and catholicity of appreciation. And so I protest against methods which tend to narrow appreciation, and especially against preference-judgments. It is so much easier to criticise than to appreciate; and the mania of delivering judgment at any price upon everything, whether appreciated or not, is a downright bad habit of thought, which breeds intolerance against unaccustomed effects and simply fossilises appreciation. Loss of flexibility, loss of independence are its inevitable results.

I said that the best and surest way of forming and developing taste is to get accustomed to the best. This will probably be ad-mitted. But it will be answered: 'Yes, but how am I to know the "best", except by comparison?' To this I would reply as follows. The hypothesis that each individual is, so to speak, a blank and has to start *ab ovo* in his experience is nonsense. He does *not*, as a rule, have to select for himself what is best; he knows it beforehand; he is told. No more than in Morals he has to discover for himself that not to steal is better than to steal, does he in Art have to find out by comparison that *Pendennis* is a better novel than a penny dread-ful, *Othello* a better play than the *Prodigal Son* or Ruysdael's and Meissonier's pictures superior to the illustrations in the *Strand Magazine* or the *Graphic*. These things he knows beforehand,

[1] [In the long footnote on p. 41. Ed.]

probably before he has ever seen or read the works. That is precisely what museums are there for. In them are to be found such works as have been strong enough to survive in the struggle for existence, to maintain themselves in the opinion, admiration and experience of centuries. They represent what has been, and still is, accepted as the 'best'. Here he can find ample material for the forming of his taste.

Finally I deny that the prime function of art-criticism is to tell us what is better and what is worse. The prime function of art-criticism is *to interpret*, to deepen individual experiences, awaking them in all their wealth in duller and less appreciative minds. If in a work there is *nothing* to interpret, the work condemns itself. If there *is*, and the interpretation succeeds, the work can very well be left to take care of itself. It does not need to be specially acclaimed as 'great' by a number of critics. It will last in its own strength and worth, unconcerned as to whether it is 'better' or 'worse' than another work—for it is GOOD.

\* \* \*

This way of looking at Æsthetics illustrates the enormous widening of its field which has taken place within the last thirty years. The subject-matter with which it has to deal, has, in this direction alone, without mentioning developments along other lines, been extended almost indefinitely. Æsthetics can no longer be satisfied with the investigation, either dialectically or by superficially empirical methods, of any one supposedly absolute Beauty. It stands face to face with the alarmingly complex and bewilderingly multiform world of actual æsthetic experiences and art products. But here arises the first difficulty: what is to become of the theoretical unification of this intricate mass of facts? How is it possible to arrive at that co-ordination of phenomena which a theory requires, if the phenomena themselves are pronounced to be incomparable with each other? How can any basis for a principle be found, if the principle is to take account of all the subtlest shadings of difference, to embrace them all and yet allow latitude for individual variations? The co-ordination was easy enough, if you simply took certain buildings, statues and pictures, measured them, found a common ratio and labelled this ratio the criterion of the beautiful. Those buildings, statues and paintings which did not conform to it were blithely disregarded, or simply pronounced less perfect than the others. There you had a unification in the simplest conceivable manner. But on the modern view, which has become chary of comparisons, which would even refuse to set up any special work of acknowledged excellence as a standard of perfection, the whole subject-matter of Æsthetics seems to fall asunder in innumerable fragments of concrete experience. If I may not even compare two marble statues in point of Beauty, how am I to find any common denominator at all which makes them commensurable with each other? Yet some point of view common to all facts is essential for a theory. The orbits of the planets and the trajectory of a cannon-ball, however dissimilar in many respects a planet and a cannon-ball may be, yet offer features which makes it possible to subsume both phenomena under the law of gravity. And Æsthetics requires, in order to exist as a study, some co-ordination, some subsumption of the particular facts under a common point of view. *In fact the development of this point of view is equivalent to the development of Æsthetics.* It was partly this theoretical preoccupation which postulated the existence of 'absolute beauty' as a higher and independent entity. And Æsthetics in its modern development has constantly shifted the standpoint of its speculations in an attempt to embrace the whole of its constantly expanding subject-matter.

I have recorded the failure of earlier methods of attacking the problem not with any intention of either discrediting the vast amount of thought expended on the subject, or of denying the undoubted contributions they made to the development of Æsthetics, but simply to throw into relief the remarkable advance made possible by the next radical change of point of view. Without those earlier speculations this change could hardly have imposed itself as inevitably as it has done. This further extension of the field of Æsthetics has been the result of directing attention to the effects of Beauty instead of enquiring about its nature or causes. Since the questions 'What is Beauty?', 'What causes Beauty?', 'How do we recognise something beautiful as such?' remained insoluble, the only remaining line of attack was the *problem of its effect*. The questions now asked were not about Beauty in itself, but about Beauty *in relation to* the mind of the spectator, listener, or (if you will forgive the ugly but convenient term) the recipient. The centre of gravity was thus shifted and the problem of the recipient consciousness affected by Beauty became the starting-point of modern Æsthetics.

If we recall that the first beginnings of such a new conception of æsthetic problems are to be found among English thinkers of the eighteenth century, it seems all the more regrettable that the subject should have fallen into neglect in this country to the extent that it has. What, in fact, makes Burke's *Inquiry into the Sublime and Beautiful* in large measure still so readable, and gives it occasionally almost the appearance of a modern work, is the space and importance he gives to the subjective aspect of the questions he discusses, and his contemporaries Hogarth and Lord Kaimes, as well as the *Discourses* of Sir Joshua Reynolds, convey a similar impression. It is true, of course, that none of these writers, as little as many who followed them and were under their influence, Winkelmann or Lessing, for instance, actually realised the possibilities of such a new conception. Their main endeavours were still directed to the solution of the old conundrums. Even in antiquity we find in Plato, Plotinus, Philostratus, and especially in Aristotle, the beginnings of a psychological analysis of æsthetic effects,[1] but there too it is subordinate to their preoccupation with absolute Beauty as an independent entity. It was Kant who, himself in so many respects indebted to English thought, definitely placed Æsthetics upon an almost exclusively subjective basis. And the development of Psychology as an autonomous science has

[1] Cf. O. Külpe, 'Die Anfänge der psychologischen Æsthetik bei den Griechen', *Philosophische Abhandlungen*, Berlin, 1906.

further accentuated this subjective tendency—despite opposition from the post-Kantian systems of metaphysics which tended to revive older dialectical methods of æsthetic speculation. How long and difficult the transition to the new standpoint has been, is clear from the work of Fechner, who has been called the 'father of modern Æsthetics'. His aim was to deal with Æsthetics, as he put it, 'from below', i.e. empirically-psychologically, instead of 'from above', i.e. dialectically. But in spite of this conscious endeavour his attempts to find measurable 'criteria' and 'causes' of Beauty are, at bottom, a continuation of the older traditions.

The subject-matter of modern 'psychological' Æsthetics is, as I said, the æsthetic impression upon the recipient consciousness, the study of the effects produced by the contemplation, primarily, of works of Art. It is the advantages attendant upon this conception of its task, as well as the expansion of its purview, that I now wish to indicate.

(1) Firstly, we may note that the study of æsthetic impression affords a standpoint for the co-ordination of æsthetic facts such as could not possibly be obtained from exclusive preoccupation with objective definitions or criteria of Beauty. The discovery in the objective world of Art of a common feature of sufficient concreteness to make it applicable both to all works and to each one separately cannot reasonably be hoped for. Theoretical unification of the empirical facts on purely objective lines is either so vague or so artificial as to be practically valueless. But in the psychical processes constituting the æsthetic impression the various arts and particular works of art may find a common meeting-ground. It may be that common to all æsthetic impressions, derived from works however divergent, there are features which represent the essence of æsthetic impression in general and thus offer a common denominator for the most varied æsthetic effects. If such a feature exists, it must be of a nature to allow the fullest scope to additional differentiations due to the peculiarities either of the work itself or of the personality of the recipient. In this way it might be possible to formulate a principle or principles which would cover all

experiences, without obliterating the indisputable differences between different effects, and without becoming abstract to the extent of applying to practically everything, both æsthetic and extra-æsthetic. Such features of the æsthetic impression—to mention three or four by way of example without criticising them in any way—are: Kant's 'disinterested pleasure', Schiller's 'illusion-theory', recently developed by K. Lange into the theory of 'conscious self-deception', various theories (such as Grant Allen's or Herbert Spencer's) amounting in substance to the statement that 'Beauty produces a maximum of pleasure with a minimum of pain or psychic expenditure', H. R. Marshall's view of the 'relative permanence of æsthetic pleasure', or the at present so very prevalent theory of 'Einfühlung' or 'self-abandonment to the art-object': all these represent one or more features of the æsthetic effect, realised more or less completely in face of any work of art, before a painting as well as before a statue, a piece of music, a novel, a tragedy, a building, etc. At the same time the possibility is provided for that in each case the actual content of the impression varies, and need not in any way be identical in degree, quality, duration or in the way it is produced. Yet the feature is sufficiently definite and circumscribed in its range as not to apply to a coal-scuttle or a clothes-brush as well as to a statue or a cathedral (which is the weakness of objective criteria, such as 'the golden section').

(2) Secondly, the study of æsthetic effects gets over a difficulty which proved an inseparable obstacle to 'objective' investigations of Beauty. We commonly speak of a tragedy, a building, etc., as sublime, a comedy or story as comical, a picture or poem as pretty rather than beautiful. These qualifications of Beauty were known theoretically as 'modifications' or 'categories' of the beautiful, and the 'absolutely beautiful' was supposed to comprise both the beautiful in the narrower sense and the sublime, the tragic, comic, pretty, touching, etc., as its sub-divisions. Now, as might be expected, the characterisation of the beautiful in terms of objective qualities frequently did not square with the qualities of the sub-

lime or the comic, etc. (quite apart from the initial difficulty of deciding whether a thing was to be regarded as beautiful or as sublime). The result was that contradictory qualities were often ascribed to the beautiful and to the sublime, of which Burke again affords illustrations. While claiming smallness, smoothness, gradual curvature, elegance, brightness for the beautiful, he is forced to mention vastness, obscurity, power, infinity, suddenness, difficulty, etc., as characteristics of the sublime. Even the downright ugly or grotesque, exercising, as it often does, a powerful æsthetic fascination, had to be taken unto account and became a fertile source of theoretical trouble. It developed into a special problem of the relation of Ugliness to Beauty.[1] Ugliness was sometimes included in the beautiful, sometimes excluded from it and treated separately, sometimes its existence was flatly denied. Needless to say, this introduced the most hopeless chaos into the conception of the 'absolutely beautiful', which was supposed to contain all these categories, and the result was a further disintegration of the subject-matter of Æsthetics. This is a difficulty which for modern psychological Æsthetics can hardly be said to exist. It is, of course, far from denying the existence of such categories, as little as it denies the differentiations of the various arts. But from its subjective point of view it is in a position to effect a subsumption of all the modifications of the beautiful under the general conception of the *æsthetic*—not because all these effects are alike, but because they all contain, though in various degrees and combinations, the main features of the essence of æsthetic effect in general. Naturally, the ultimate test of the validity of any such principle is its ability to do justice to all the different forms of experience comprehended under the term *æsthetic*. In modern æsthetic literature, this term has, for ordinary purposes, almost completely superseded the older and so much narrower expression 'beautiful'. And in its very vagueness it is really much more precise, more easily applicable to experiences which one would often hesitate to call definitely beautiful or sublime or touching, etc.

[1] Cf. K. Rosenkranz, *Æsthetik des Hässlichen*, Königsberg, 1853.

(3) Lastly, modern Æsthetics avoids by reason of its standpoint the rock on which all objective theories have stranded: the lack of a consensus of opinion. As I have already discussed the point, I need not enlarge upon it here. What was absolutely fatal to such theories of beauty is relatively immaterial to the psychological study of æsthetic problems. For the fact that opinions differ (which is tantamount to a disproof of the objective position, since it denies the supposed objective, and therefore demonstrable, Beauty of a thing) indicates for psychological theory merely a difference, sometimes a deficiency, in the psychical processes of the individual percipient. And the superiority of this view is that it not only safeguards the validity of its principles against accidental and very natural divergencies of opinion, but positively makes room for them, regards them as facts to be expected and in themselves perfectly intelligible. Let us for argument's sake (taking an extreme case and over-simplifying it) assume that the Venus of Milo represents the 'golden section' or any other ratio supposed to be the essence of beauty. Now a Bodokuto or a Hottentot might fail to see the Beauty of the Venus. He might still do so, even after the ratio had been mathematically demonstrated to him *ad oculos*. Theoretically he thereby disproves the statement that the golden section is *ipso facto* beautiful. The explanation that the Venus probably does not tally with his ideal of feminine Beauty, though apparently quite rational, does not mend matters from the point of view of the objective theory. Such things as ideals of feminine Beauty, types, associations, memories, custom, etc., do not enter into its purview. Psychological Æsthetics, on the other hand, not only finds the explanation quite intelligible, but can even undertake to show how and why this should be the cause of disagreement. But then it can afford to take this attitude; for the Hottentot's failure to appreciate the Venus leaves her Beauty entirely unaffected. Hence that vast field of investigation into the causes of differences of opinion, into racial, climatic, social, educational, religious and other influences, both on the formation and development of arts and art-forms, and on the evolution of appreciation

and taste, is an integral part of modern Æsthetics. Its indebtedness in this respect to the History of Civilisation, of Religion and Mythology, to Ethnology, Sociology and Archæology can hardly be over-stated. Yet all these were fields of study which older Æsthetics at least theoretically disregarded and left untouched.

The psychological analysis of æsthetic effect is, of course, *firstly*, of an introspective nature: our own experiences, of which we alone possess first-hand evidence, furnish the bulk of the subject-matter to be examined. But Æsthetics cannot remain satisfied with such detached and necessarily inco-ordinate conclusions as those drawn from individual experience, in which the factor of un-conscious self-deception and auto-suggestion cannot be excluded even by the most carefully cultivated introspection. Hence it is led *secondly* to the examination of data obtained from others by means of observation, exchange of opinion and common partici-pation in æsthetic experiences. Here again the most easily obtain-able and most trustworthy evidence is that of individuals of approximately the same degree of development and general psychical constitution as ourselves, that is, of our contemporaries, with whom we can come into personal contact and whom we may most reasonably suppose to resemble ourselves. In this way we can correct personal idiosyncrasies and supplement defects of which each of us is inevitably aware. Only *thirdly*, can Æsthetics take account of the testimony of persons either further removed from ourselves in general development, or separated by racial, social and cultural conditions of life. Thus the æsthetic experiences of children, which undoubtedly differ more than is usually as-sumed from those of adults, and those of primitives and savages, which formerly were often grievously misunderstood by being interpreted too much on the analogy of our own, are brought within the purview of Æsthetics. It must not, however, be thought that all this analysis and investigation can be successfully carried on without constant reference to the objective world of art-products. On the contrary, it is essential to preserve continual contact with the forms of Art, from which, after all, most æsthetic impressions are derived. Differentiations of effect must be considered in relation to differentiations of the objective forms which produce them. It has been a failing of some work on Æsthetics, carried out on exclusively subjective-psychological lines, to have lost this contact; and the result has been accounts of emotions, pleasure, perception, etc., in general, instead of research into *æsthetic* perception, *æsthetic* pleasure, *æsthetic* emotions; that is, the loss of a distinctively æsthetic point of view. Thus, *fourthly*, the study of the objective features of art, *not* as objective characteristics of Beauty, as in older theories, but always in relation to their æsthetic effect, opens up an avenue to the understanding of art-forms themselves as well as to what might be called the technical side of Art. By this means the whole world of Art, as an objective phenomenon, and Art-history as the tale of its evolution, finds its place within Æsthetics. A not unimportant addition to the study is the use of æsthetic experiment, especially with the simplest and most elementary æsthetic objects, such as lines, simple figures, colours, rhythms, melodies, etc., where by the arbitrary modification of objective features corresponding modifications of effect can be examined. This again, it need hardly be said, must not be confused with older attempts to establish certain proportions or harmonies as the essence of the Beautiful *without consideration of the resulting effects*.

We must now ask whether this conception of Æsthetics is capable of performing all the tasks which might reasonably be expected of the subject, whether from the point of view of *æsthetic effect* all the facts can be covered. We must realise that, if this proves not to be the case, if a residue of problems is left out of account, this point of view does not represent the highest synthesis and co-ordination of all the facts. We should consequently have to cast about for a more comprehensive standpoint which would ensure the inclusion of such phenomena.

Now there is a whole group of phenomena, highly important phenomena, which cannot properly be subsumed under the heading of æsthetic effect: the phenomena of *artistic production*. It is only natural that the success which has so far attended psychological research into æsthetic effect should have led to enthusiastic exaggeration both of the purely psychological method and of the importance to be attached to the analysis of æsthetic impression. Hence the attempt has been made to force artistic production too under the unifying point of view of æsthetic effect. The possibility of studying the technical aspect of Art, and the development of objective art-forms, from this point of view led to the assumption that it was feasible to try to understand artistic production and the processes of artistic creation from the same standpoint. It was, in fact, assumed that production was a kind of prospective æsthetic effect, and that what held good for the latter was directly applicable to the former. Yet in spite of the indisputable and fundamental connection between the two sets of phenomena, we have *prima facie* no reason to suppose that production essentially involves factors of æsthetic effect; or that æsthetic enjoyment of effect is the same as the proverbial 'joy of production'; or that the attitude of the artist towards work yet to be produced corresponds (even prospectively) to the attitude of a recipient towards the finished production of another. To some extent æsthetic appreciation does imply *a kind of* production, unconscious and predetermined; even as production *in some sense* involves prospective æsthetic impression. But notwithstanding this interpenetrating or overlapping of the two sets of phenomena, the one cannot straightway be subordinated to the other without the risk of not doing justice to either: to the nature of the artist and the manner of his production, or to the essence of æsthetic contemplation. Here again Æsthetics stands in danger of forcing the facts to suit the theory, i.e. to suit the scientific necessity of theoretical unification. The recognition of artistic production as in some measure an independent sphere produces a cleavage in Æsthetics. If this sphere is to be included within its purview, the conception of Æsthetics has to be widened and its co-ordinating point of view raised.

Even then, the whole subject-matter of Æsthetics has not been exhausted. Neither æsthetic impression nor artistic production, the two main branches of modern æsthetic study, complete the whole circle of æsthetic experiences in human life. Even if we extend it, as speculative theories traditionally did, beyond Art into the domain of Nature, we do not thereby push beyond the confines of æsthetic effects; for the impression of the Beauty of Nature is not fundamentally different from that produced by works of Art, though the inclusion of natural Beauties may counteract exaggeratedly *artistic* theories in Æsthetics. Yet beyond even this furthest extension to which Æsthetics has so far ventured, there lies a residue of æsthetic experiences which cannot be classed either under effect or production, though in a sense they simultaneously partake of both. At the present time they cannot even be said to be generally recognised. If I refer to them here in the most sketchy manner, and even at the risk of some obscurity, I do so, because it appears to me the widest and most comprehensive enlargement of Æsthetics, of which the study is at present capable. This field has been called by a recent writer[1] the sphere of 'æsthetic culture'. It is a field which belongs neither to the æsthetic impression as derived from works of art, nor to the conscious production of such works, nor yet to the æsthetic effect of natural objects; and yet it combines in constantly shifting combinations all these various aspects, and in its realisation assumes a practical importance in the shaping of our actual conduct which the other spheres can only claim in the most indirect way, through the mediating function of Art.

Pater wrote of the æsthetic spirit pervading all things that partake in any degree of artistic qualities: the furniture of our houses, life itself, gesture and speech, and the details of daily intercourse; 'these also, for the wise, being susceptible of a suavity and charm, caught from the way in which they are done, which gives to them a worth in themselves; wherein, indeed, lies what is valuable and justly attractive . . . which elevates the trivialities of speech, and manner and dress, into "ends in themselves" and gives them a

---

[1] E. Meumann, 'Die Grenzen der psychologischen Æsthetik', *Philosophische Abhandlungen*, Berlin, 1906.

mysterious grace and attractiveness in the doing of them'.[1] Our whole life is, indeed, saturated with this æsthetic charm, which, however despised by some and neglected by most, yet exhales an aroma so ethereal that it hardly obtrudes itself upon our attention, though we may at once become sensible of its loss. Its most evident expression it finds in those external conditions which we consciously induce in order to enforce it upon our sensibility, in those things of our daily existence which Pater mentioned: our houses, our rooms, our furniture, our tools; even ourselves, in the externalities of personal manner and bearing, we endeavour to invest with that special attractiveness to which we cannot apply any other epithet but 'æsthetic'. Yet all these are but *external* conditions. They either satisfy some inward craving for æsthetic satisfaction or minister to the æsthetic expression of some inward impulse. It is the INWARD world, of which all these external circumstances are but the reflection, which is essentially the world of 'æsthetic culture'. And from this inner world, æsthetic culture is carried over not only into the material features of our existence, but also transfused into our spiritual needs and strivings. Thus æsthetic considerations enter into educational questions, religious convictions, intellectual pursuits, into our own conduct and individual acts and the way we evaluate the actions of our fellow-creatures. Our whole psychic life is permeated with this mysterious æsthetic culture, and our general attitude towards experience, our complete outlook upon life in general, is not infrequently more of an æsthetic than of a practical, scientific or ethical nature. Individuals undoubtedly differ much in the persistency and definiteness of this attitude. Some realise it intensely only at rare moments, before a work of art, before some great event. With others it is habitual, and sometimes so deeply rooted that it supersedes almost all other points of view, going out to even the most trifling objects or circumstances with a kindly sympathy, as to a thing of interest and indefinable grace. It is precisely this capacity for sympathetic interest and, in a sense, impersonal

[1] *The Renaissance*, 1873, p. 143.

curiosity, which distinguishes the artist from the mere sentimental dreamer and from the ordinary prosaic mind. Yet everyone, even the most prosaic individual, possesses in some degree an æsthetic outlook on experience. What we call tact is essentially a form of behaviour actuated by æsthetic habits of thought and feeling. What might be termed the education of the heart, as distinct from the education of the intellect, means the development of our æsthetic sensitiveness to life. Culture, as distinct from learning, education in its fullest sense, pure humanity, with what is best and without what is worst in human nature, rests fundamentally upon such an education of the heart, upon such an æsthetic philosophy of life.

It has been said that most great men are great actors. The usual interpretation of this is, of course, the vulgar detraction of great personalities into hypocritical intriguers and clever shams, who merely 'act' for their own advantage and whose professions of personal conviction are simply a pretence. But the saying admits of another interpretation. And in this sense it is true not only of great men but, though in lesser degree, of almost all men. There are many who are 'actors', not in the sense that they *pretend* to do and think before others what they would neither do nor think in the privacy of their own chamber (the usual false significance attributed to 'acting'), but in the sense that they perform perfectly natural and spontaneous acts with so clear a perception of their nature, their value and their sensuous, concrete effectiveness that these acts assume for them an intrinsic importance (quite apart from ultimate aims or results), an importance such as acts, done unconsciously or only with some definite purpose in view, can never assume. In the doing of them they experience a kind of separation within themselves, a doubling of consciousness, as if they were two individuals, of which one acts while the other looks on, criticises and enjoys, with the free and impartial interest and the satisfaction which the artist feels in the production of his own handiwork. Thus they combine in themselves the threefold aspect of artist, work of art and spectator, an exceedingly complex mental state, common enough in the actor, but realised in actual life, too, more often than we are inclined to think. The result is a curious enhancement of the acts, of the most trivial as of the most sublime. They are invested with a value as ends in themselves, done for their own sake, with a devotion and detachment impossible in acts performed for the sake of further ends or ulterior reasons. Perhaps such acts represent, in their freedom from personal motives and the perfect abandonment to their performance, the highest kind of behaviour of which a human being is capable: deeds of heroism as well as the simplest acts of kindness, always done with the full intensity of the whole personality behind them. To realise this is the ideal of æsthetic culture. Nothing can be further from the mind of such an 'actor' than the self-complacency or vulgar ostentation which the ignorant so easily attribute to his conduct. For æsthetic 'doing for the doing's sake' calls into play the full powers of the personality only in the measure that it overcomes narrow motives of individual advantage or exhibitions of personal vanity.

This attitude towards our own conduct can also operate in appraising the conduct of others. We do not invariably judge our own actions from the exclusive standpoint of morality; and we do not always, or even habitually, estimate the acts of others by reference to their moral excellence or deficiency. The fact is, as it seems to me, that many acts, especially deeds of great power, of enthusiasm, passion or heroism, deeds, that is, of the highest importance both to the individual performer and often to others, are precisely acts which escape ethical evaluation. That they *can* be subjected to moral criteria is not, of course, denied; but the point is that, since they are not performed from any distinctly ethical motive, a merely moral judgment falsifies the whole position. It depreciates their intrinsic worth and impoverishes their essentially human value. Even a crime may, to this view, be a 'great' crime, while a perfectly moral act may repel us by its sterility, its want of vivifying warmth or manifested livingness. Generally speaking, the conduct of our contemporaries concerns our personal interests too closely to allow (except in particular cases and in particular individuals) this full æsthetic appreciation. It is towards historical personages[1] that it operates most freely and comprehensively. Here, unblinded by personal interest, we can appreciate characters who realised this ideal of æsthetic culture. The great men of Athens or the Renaissance,[2] Pericles or Plato, Pico della Mirandola, Leonardo da Vinci, Lorenzo the Magnificent or Julius II, men of the stamp of Goethe, were men of such æsthetic culture, *human* beings compared with whom some of the greatest intellects, when divested of the glamour of their achievements in special spheres, are but insignificant pigmies. For these were often *nothing but* great thinkers, inventors or statesmen. For all their power of intellect or will, they lack that marvellously many-sided and yet perfectly balanced inward largeness of those *human* heroes. Even after subtracting our admiration for the statesmanship of Pericles, for the vast metaphysical imagination of Plato, the sublime Utopias of Pico, the encyclopædic knowledge of Leonardo, the lyric poetry of Goethe, there remains a residue of such monumental, and yet such human, humanity, that it towers over the petty existences of others more famous for accuracy of learning or feats of discovery. The true heights of the human race are more truly represented in such lives than in material improvements of the conditions of existence or in contributions added to the store of knowledge. Inventions and scientific discoveries are superseded,

---

[1] For the close relation between Art and History in this respect cf. M. Dessoir: 'Beiträge zur Æsthetik' III, *Archiv für Philosophie*, II.Abt. vol. V, 1899, pp. 464–72.

[2] Cf. J. A. Symonds, *Renaissance in Italy*, vol. III, *The Fine Arts*, London, 1877, p. 4: 'The speech of the Italians of that epoch, their social habits, their ideal of manners, their standard of morality, the estimate they formed of men, were alike conditioned and qualified by art. It was an age of splendid ceremonies and magnificent parade, when the furniture of houses, the armour of soldiers, the dress of citizens, the pomp of war, and the pageantry of festival were invariably and inevitably beautiful. On the meanest articles of domestic utility, cups and platters, door-panels and chimney-pieces, coverlets for beds and lids of linen-chests, a wealth of artistic invention was lavished by innumerable craftsmen, no less skilled in technical details than distinguished by rare taste.'

they become the obsolete trivialities of succeeding generations and their originators die but for text-books and scientific annals. But such men remain as living monuments, and contact with them an ever fresh spring of encouragement and imperishable vitality. Because their greatness lies in their æsthetic culture, in the fullest sense of this term, so our full understanding of them is impossible except æsthetically. And, on an infinitely smaller scale, what we ourselves do or feel or experience æsthetically, for the sake of doing, feeling or experiencing it, persists and forms a more valuable addition to our life than any carefully laid and executed plans of personal interest, or even the treasures of abstract learning we may accumulate. For everything else is a means to living; this alone is an end in itself, a fragment of concretely realised Life.

The bearing of such æsthetic culture (to use this short term) upon our practical existence, the intermingling of such distinctively æsthetic aspects of life with those of a practical or ethical nature, the innumerable forms which this culture assumes, are as much a field of study as æsthetic effect or artistic production. And just as production cannot be subordinated to effect or vice versa, so this æsthetic culture cannot be subordinated to either. It remains a distinct, though related, field of enquiry. The unification of the subject which was already lost by including artistic production in the domain of Æsthetics seems, then, farther removed than ever by the inclusion of æsthetic culture. The question now is this: Is there any point of view from which Æsthetics can succeed in co-ordinating these distinct spheres and in subordinating them all to one comprehensive conception? This would be the highest synthesis of which the discipline is capable.

To this I answer: There *is* such a conception. *It is the conception of Æsthetics as the systematic study of æsthetic consciousness.* This manifests itself in æsthetic appreciation, as well as in artistic production; and in the broad, less easily definable, field of æsthetic culture. It may be regarded as distinct from, though co-ordinate with, the practical, scientific and ethical consciousness, as they reveal themselves in practical life, scientific constructions and ethical ideals.

H

And thus Æsthetics shares with the various studies treating of practical problems, with the natural sciences, and with Moral Philosophy, the task of investigating and comprehending human Life, in all its various manifestations and forms.

This is no mere matter of words. The expression 'æsthetic consciousness' is not just a phrase, and the unification of the æsthetic field of enquiry by this term not simply verbal. To the term 'æsthetic consciousness' there corresponds something which actually and really exists in sufficient definiteness, in spite of its fluctuating forms, to allow of its being grasped and understood. It is, of course, one of the tasks of Æsthetics to elaborate and develop its meaning far beyond the superficial sketch which I now offer.

By 'consciousness' I mean not so much what Psychology understands by the word in its strict sense, as a more or less fixed and habitual mental attitude towards things in general, towards life, experience and the world at large. It must be borne in mind that our usual outlook upon things, by reason of which they appear to us as things of practical utility, as scientific objects, as sources of æsthetic enjoyment, is a subjective attitude which may or may not be specially conditioned by the objective qualities of the thing in question. This is especially true of æsthetic objects. When we call a thing æsthetic, the reason is to be sought as much, nay even more, in the subjective attitude of the recipient as in the objective features of the thing itself. Everything can, at least theoretically, become for me an æsthetic object, whether it be meant to affect me in this way or not. As a matter of experience, most things are capable of 'appearing' to us in different ways, although generally a railway train is more likely to be looked upon as an object of practical use, while a statue or piece of music will, by reason of its objective qualities, more easily produce an æsthetic than a practical or scientific response. Interchanges of attitude in respect of these individual things are, however, common enough.

1. The least distinctive attitude is undoubtedly the *practical consciousness*. Fortunately there is no need to enlarge on it, since we all have first-hand experience of what it means. It represents, on

the one hand, that purely unsophisticated outlook upon the universe which Flaubert ironically characterised as the belief that 'le soleil est fait pour éclairer la terre'. It is formed by the instinctive conviction that the individual is the culminating point of the world and that everything else is there for his personal benefit or as a means to his existence. Even the thought that there are other worlds besides his own has something unpleasant for him, because they are necessarily unconnected with his presence in this world. On the other hand, however, the practical consciousness is a complex conglomeration of the less primitive conceptions of Science, Ethics, Religion, and very largely also of Æsthetics; and this makes it so intricate and many-faceted that it is impossible to describe it, even in the most casual way, in a few words. One thing, however, may be said. All its ingredients are tinged in their combination by the peculiarly anthropocentric view alluded to above. Considerations of utility, the pursuit of private or practical interests, the perfectly legitimate participation in the struggle for existence are expressions of this anthropocentric attitude, which conceives of the individual as a personal agent concerned primarily with his own welfare to which most other things have reference. It is a kind of teleological conception of life on the lower plane of utilitarian ends.

2. With the *scientific consciousness* the case is very different. This attitude towards the universe is one which is by no means natural and obvious, even to such a scientific age as ours. It is, no doubt, true that our whole mental life is now so permeated with Science and its conceptions, that an existence without them may appear to us most *un*natural. Yet the non-scientific man's idea of the scientific point of view is either, in accordance with the general tendency of the practical consciousness, predominantly utilitarian, or it combines scientific notions in the most convenient way with his own teleological outlook, and thereby falsifies the genuine scientific standpoint. The *non*-teleological conception of things, as Science formulates it on its exclusively intellectual basis, appears to him on closer acquaintance unbearably cold and materialistic.

Even if it temporarily satisfies his curiosity, it remains essentially
alien to him, for Science looks back, where he wants to look forward, and Science gives rational explanations, where he expects
hopes and assurances for the future. The high idealism of 'knowledge for the sake of knowledge', which far more than the practical utilisation of scientific discoveries characterises the scientific
attitude, however much applauded in theory, remains unintelli-
gible to the practical mind in practice. The fact that Science
admits no purpose nor any teleological consideration to enter its
concepts, is the gulf which separates it from the practical view of
the world as an arena where wills, purposes, projects, intentions
and interests engage in combat.

Unfortunately the claim of Science to furnish the only *objectively*
valid account of the world blinds, not only the 'man in the street',
but sometimes the scientist himself to the fact that Science is
essentially a *subjective* point of view, a 'form of consciousness' in
the above sense, one of several ways of interpreting Nature. 'The
aspiration to be "scientific" ', says William James, 'is such an idol
of the tribe to the present generation, is so sucked in with his
mother's milk by everyone of us, that we find it hard to conceive
of a creature who should not feel it, and harder still to treat it
freely as the altogether peculiar and one-sided subjective interest
which it is.'[1] As such a subjective interest it aims at the rational
explanation of phenomena by reason of antecedent configurations
of facts and conditions; or if I may venture to put it (inadequately
no doubt) into a short formula: the *scientific consciousness is retrospectively explanatory or causal*, causal in the sense of an efficient, but
not of a final cause. This conception only apparently conflicts with
the pragmatic notion of the essential usefulness of Science, with its
justification by application and by its use in the transformation of
our experience. For its power to deal prospectively with the emer-
gencies of experience is derived from its retrospective analysis of
already experienced phenomena.

[1] *Principles of Psychology*, New York, 1890, II, p. 640.

3. The direct opposite to the scientific point of view is the *ethical attitude*. As Science represents a 'construction' of the universe in terms of *causality*, so Ethics is the interpretation of existence in terms of *finality*. It deals with action, conduct, personality, not with an eye on the causes which produced them, but always with reference to the realisation of an end, of a *summum bonum* variously defined. Whereas Psychology formulates its conception of human personality as a sequence of states of consciousness, causally developed from antecedents, and treats of it in a purely descriptive manner, Ethics regards it as an individual agent tending towards certain ends and working in the direction of a certain goal. The scientific attitude is *retrospective*, the ethical is *prospective*. Even when judging actions it only *appears* to go backwards, in order to gain from the vantage-point of the motive a prospective view of the act and its consequences. In so far as it has reference to *human* will and purpose only, it leaves Nature, apart from Man, out of account. But in its wider view of the universe as the realisation of some underlying *final* cause, and as the gradual unfolding of some teleological idea, it comprises everything in a vast conception of a morally constituted world. The antithesis between Science and Ethics lies precisely in the non-teleological character of the one and the prospective finality of the other. And it is this latter point which forms the contact between the ethical and the practical attitude. The famous and futile quarrels between Religion and Science, and the endless discussions on the freedom or determination of the will, bear sufficient testimony to the antagonism between the ethical and the scientific points of view. Yet the opposition is only apparent. For the two contending views are merely two different interpretations of the same fact, two distinct subjective attitudes.

4. And now my task is to define the *æsthetic consciousness* and distinguish it from these others.

The differences between it and either the ethical or the scientific attitude are fairly evident, especially in the most elaborate and distinctive form of æsthetic consciousness, namely that which pro-

duces or appreciates a work of art. A work of art unquestionably
has antecedents in the scientific sense of the word. The evolution
of its conception in the mind of the artist is the *subjective* aspect of
these antecedents. Besides these it has also *objective* antecedents: the
various art-forms preceding this special work and in a sense making it possible; the evolution of the particular art the work belongs
to; the development of technique; the intellectual, social and
other factors leading to its production. The æsthetic effect, on the
other hand, has *its* antecedents in the qualifications and peculiarities of the recipient personality. It may have final results, too, in
the sense of moral consequences, in its bearing upon personal conduct, in the shaping of personal ideals, etc. But none of these
points are of an *æsthetic* nature. *Æsthetically* a work of art has
neither antecedents nor final results.[1] Æsthetically the production
of an art-object does not go beyond the realisation of the artistic
conception in the work, nor is the æsthetic impression a result, to
some extent independent of the work which produced it (as the
moral consequences of an act assume an importance and live in the
strength of their own reality, independently of their proximate
causes). Æsthetic response remains centred on the work, drawing
its enjoyment from it and reflecting it back upon it. That the other
points of view are possible is, of course, a truism: the History of
Art, sociological and ethical studies of Art, Æsthetics itself, are
evidence of that. But the æsthetic attitude is neither scientific nor
ethical. It rests in the work without transcending it either forwards
or backwards. It is, in distinction to the formulas adopted before,
neither retrospective nor prospective, but *immanent*; neither
explanatory nor final, but *contemplative*. And this is true not
only of Art, but of Nature and Life when these are viewed
æsthetically.

   This immanent contemplativeness of the æsthetic attitude is the
magical wand which invests all things it touches with a charm and

---

[1] Cf. Schiller, *Das Glück*:
   'Aber das Glückliche siehest du nicht, das Schöne nicht werden,
   Fertig von Ewigkeit her steht es vollendet vor dir.'

interest, which considered as products of antecedent causes, or as means to a purpose, they cannot possibly possess. It gives a plasticity and relief to objects and experiences which they inevitably lose in the long perspectives of scientific or ethical vistas. An action may be damaging or beneficial in its consequences; it may be inspired by good or bad motives; or it may represent the final link in a long chain of psychic states, the result of physiological disturbances, the concomitant phenomenon of certain emotional conditions. But it may also be the concrete expression of a concentrated vitality. The desperate leap of a prisoner for freedom, the wild rush of an attack, the deliberate act of taking one's life, may be ethically approved or condemned, they may be scientifically analysed. But only to the æsthetic consciousness is revealed what the act meant to the doer, the overflowing fullness of living energy and the clenched resolve of its performance. Not so much to live happily rather than miserably, or to lead a godly rather than a wicked life, but to *live*, to force life of the highest quality in its deepest and intensest form into the span of a human existence, is an ideal purely æsthetic. Æsthetic consciousness discovers that innumerable acts are daily done, not for the sake of practical utility nor in conscious observance of ethical postulates, but because the doing of them was accompanied by that peculiar sense of enjoyment in doing them well, with all the strength, perfection and grace that could be imparted to them. So deeds of heroism may be achieved, not for glory, nor for use, nor even from distinctly realised altruistic motives, but for the sake of that feeling of intoxicating fullness of life which springs from the concentration of one's whole self into the performance of an act. It is this illuminating of the trivial and the great things of existence with the grace of being well done which is the privilege of the æsthetic consciousness. Again it is Pater who found the most concise formulation: 'Not the fruit of experience, but experience itself, is an end in itself.' Perhaps this conception could explain many lives passed in sorrow and existences which outwardly failed and yet inwardly possessed untold wealth.

Another twofold characteristic of the æsthetic attitude as distinct from the scientific and the ethical is its *sensuousness* and *individual concreteness* as opposed to their *generalisations* and *abstractness*. The individual objects or facts with which Science or Ethics deals are to them instances, test-cases, experimental illustrations of some principle, theory or construction. They either corroborate it or by their contradiction necessitate its enlargement or recasting. But æsthetically, an object is always an individual of unique complexion and character. In proportion to the precision and sensitiveness of the receptive mind it becomes incomparable to other objects, however closely related or similar. This individualising and isolating tendency of æsthetic consciousness is one of the fundamental causes of the frequent conflict between it and the predominantly scientific mind, which in accordance with its essential constitution must always compare, group, relate and inter-connect whatever comes under its observation. This feature of æsthetic appreciation is, of course, the natural result of its characteristic contemplativeness and immanence. So is the emphasis laid upon the outward sensuous appearance of things. It is the *manner* of doing, thinking, feeling more than the doing, thinking or feeling itself; or it is, to use the time-honoured though misleading distinction, the *form* rather than the *content* which assumes such importance for the æsthetic mind. For the purposes of conveying meaning through language, or of expressing an idea by means of objective forms, clearness of diction or accuracy of representation is sufficient. Hieroglyphics or pictographs answer the purpose of the former; a neatly-executed sketch or photograph fulfil the scientific requirements of the latter. But for poetry lucidity of style, or for painting the most realistic semblance, are insufficient. The sense of the value of word or line or colour, the feeling for the significance of a construction or period, for the perfection of a line-complex or a colour-scheme are things irrelevant to scientific knowledge, but paramount to æsthetic appreciation. The importance it attaches to the purely external, phenomenal side of things has often been misinterpreted as superficiality and shallowness, and the æsthetic attitude consequently despised as something rather derogatory to the 'dignity of the human mind'. But this is a misunderstanding, a misrepresentation even. For one thing æsthetic appreciation is incomparably deeper and fuller even in its appreciation of the external aspect of things than the practical 'judging by appearances'. I go further and insist that it is the *only* way in which appearances are apprehended at their full value. There is no other way in which we become actually and intensely conscious of the phenomenal aspect of things, and thereby of their beauties and perfections. The practical 'judging by appearances' is *not* apprehension of appearances as such, for their own sake, but only as indicative of whatever the practical consciousness imagines, or would like to find, behind them. In fact the æsthetic attitude avoids, by reason of its point of view, the fundamental practical error of 'judging by appearances'. This lies simply in drawing rash and erroneous inferences from a thing's appearance about its true nature, use, intention or probable results. But any such inference is foreign to æsthetic appreciation, since it is entirely incompatible with its immanence.

On the other hand, both these characteristics, sensuous concreteness and individualisation, infuse into æsthetic appreciation that peculiar human interest and element which are so conspicuously lacking in the abstract scientific standpoint and to some extent also in ethical speculation. This brings us to the difference between the *æsthetic* and the *practical* consciousness. For this human element in the æsthetic attitude is not to be confounded with the *personal* element in the practical. It is impossible to bring out in a few words the exceedingly complex nature of the æsthetic state in this respect. For though æsthetic appreciation is distinctly *in-dividual*, as opposed to the non-individual, 'objective' standpoint of Science, it is also peculiarly *impersonal* by contrast with the practical. Kant used the term 'disinterested pleasure' to denote this impersonal character, and in spite, or rather because, of its apparent contradiction in terms, it remains one of the best short descriptive formulas of the æsthetic attitude. The essential feature of this is that the æsthetic object, in so far as it is æsthetic, is temporarily severed from its relation to, and its bearing upon, our practical self. The centre of gravity is, so to speak, shifted from the personal ego to the thing contemplated. The personality is not forcibly suppressed in the way that the surgeon may force his personal sentiments into the background in the interest of scientific objectivity. But it is lost in, and spontaneously surrendered to, the object, only to live with twofold vigour and intensity in its contemplation.[1] This is the meaning of 'æsthetic objectivity', which is quite different from either scientific objectivity or the egotistical *subjectivity* of practical consciousness. One of the most striking expressions of this æsthetic peculiarity has always seemed to me the painting by Cogniet: 'Tintoretto painting his dead daughter.' There seems to be an almost surgical coldness, a scientifically objective curiosity in the face of the bearded old man as, palette in hand before the prepared canvas, he minutely scans the features of his dead child. From the practical point of view the scene is the epitome of superhuman heartlessness. In reality it represents an act of more earnest piety and greatness of heart to be thus lost in contemplation of *her* than to lose himself in heart-rending grief or wild laments.

A clear realisation of these and other distinctions between the practical, scientific and ethical consciousness, on the one hand, and the æsthetic consciousness on the other, distinctions which I have only been able to suggest in a superficial and perhaps obscure way, may help us to see the absurdity of trying to introduce into the domain of Æsthetics principles pertaining to other spheres. To identify straightway the Beautiful with the Useful, with Knowledge, with the ethically Good, or to make intellectual or moral considerations the end of æsthetic consciousness, is as mistaken as to import the ethical concept of teleological finality into the

---

[1] [Here is the germ of the principle of 'Psychical Distance' which Bullough did not fully work out, or at least did not publish, until five years later. Ed.]

scientific non-teleological world of discourse.[1]

At the same time, however, the common meeting ground of these several attitudes in human experience explains their intimate connection—a connection which older æsthetic theories could only artificially establish, or tried, equally artificially, to abolish—and calls for continuous effort to co-ordinate both the attitudes themselves and the branches of thought which deal with them. For they are all but different points of view of the same, fundamentally identical thing, namely human life and the universe we all live in.

\* \* \*

This distinction between various modes of consciousness seems to me a much more concrete, accurate and certainly more workable construction than the older distinction between 'willing', 'thinking' and 'feeling', with which Ethics, Science and Art were respectively supposed to deal. This latter view still holds its own in the popular mind, and is even to be found in recent works on Æsthetics.[2] Such a division of the human psyche into willing, thinking and feeling is a psychological monstrosity, which in no way corresponds to the facts of experience. Every thought, every emotion, every act of will implies, *ipso facto*, the two other constituents of the concrete individual. Willing without a definitely thought-of purpose and its emotional resonance, thought without the 'will to think' and the emotional factor of a purpose or interest are mere verbal and nonsensical abstractions. The distinctions I have tried to establish, on the other hand, hold good in a quite general way, even beyond the sphere to which I have here applied them, and are found to affect experiences and our conceptions of them in the minutest particulars. It would seem that all human beings are, partly constitutionally, partly owing to education, environment, etc., inclined more to the one or the other of

[1] In some such attempts the absurdity of the procedure is evident, as, for instance, in the old argument against Kepler's laws, that, since the circle is the noblest figure, the orbits of planets, being heavenly bodies, could not possibly be elliptical.

[2] E.g. in G. Fanciulli, *La coscienza estetica*, 1906.

these types of mind or mental attitudes. A great many disputes might be resolved by the frank avowal of such a difference of temperament. They seem to hold, too, in respect of philosophy. Philosophical systems are, as Nietzsche said, a kind of memoirs of their authors, the expression of their individual propensities and mental attitudes. There are, so to speak, scientific, ethical and æsthetic philosophies. The first are mainly occupied with theories of knowledge (Greek natural philosophy, the Rationalistic movement in Descartes, Spinoza, Bacon, Leibnitz and, partly, in Kant); the second are prominently ethical (Socratic or Stoic philosophy, or Kant's later position); and lastly there are philosophies which cannot be better described than æsthetic (Vedantic philosophy, Epicureanism, and certain European conceptions inspired by or under the influence of oriental thought, such as Schopenhauer's). Nietzsche's philosophy, in particular, has a distinctly æsthetic basis, which might explain why his thought is so often misunderstood, especially in academic circles, and the absurd charges of immorality which are so often preferred against him. In Schiller's recasting of Kant's rigoristic ethical ideal into the conception of the 'Schöne Seele', a transition from the ethical to the æsthetic standpoint in a philosophical construction can almost be observed in the making. It is not different with religious beliefs. There is no doubt about such religions as the Egyptian or Judaic being mainly ethical systems. The æsthetic type might, on the other hand, be illustrated by Hindooism and by its purest representative, Greek religion. On the whole, pantheistic religions seem to point to the æsthetic attitude, while the conception of a personal God, especially when armed with justice and retribution, belongs essentially to the ethical category. It would be interesting to investigate the religious beliefs of some of the greatest artists from this point of view. I believe that the large majority were open or unconscious pantheists.

\* \* \*

The monopoly which Ethics has tended to exercise in the systematisation of human aspirations and ideals does not, I believe, correspond to the actual facts of experience. There is room for an æsthetic interpretation of experience alongside it. But granted that *de facto* both the ethical and the æsthetic attitudes are realised in actual experience, what is *de jure* their mutual relationship? Ought we to consider the ethical or the æsthetic the superior attitude? Which of them is ultimately the better? The question is speculative and, apart from historical evidence, might be resolvable in both directions, according to personal inclination and ideals. *Ethics* is the outcome of *social* conditions; its origin is *communal*. If the individual did not have to live together with individuals of the same species, it would never have come into existence. Hence we find, according to the social conditions in different places and different periods of history, variations in morals which clearly point to their community origin. The *æsthetic* attitude, on the other hand, is essentially *individual*, individual both as regards the person appreciating and the object æsthetically appreciated. Hence the emphasis laid by *Ethics* upon solidarity, *esprit de corps*, communal and social necessities, and by the *æsthetic* attitude upon the aspirations and ideals of the individual being. Hence too the relatively stable consensus in ethical, compared with the relatively *un*stable consensus in æsthetic matters.

Thus the question might be formulated in another form: 'Is the individual superior to the community or the community superior to the individual?'

Here individual differences of opinion, temperament, breeding and education are bound to play a most prominent part. A general answer to such a general question is hardly ever likely to go beyond the mere expression of personal views and wishes. I do not think that the problem in this absolute form *can* be solved. The decision in concrete cases depends so entirely upon concrete factors. It depends on the value of the community and on the value of the individual. I confess, nevertheless, that personally I incline to the view that the individual is superior to the community, that human progress has always been achieved by individuals, not collectively. It is not the mass which pushes individuals into progress, but individuals who lead the masses on to advancing paths. I do not thereby intend any disparagement of the community. It is a most valuable reserve or capital for the individual to fall back upon, and the very condition and basis of his advance (though it may under certain circumstances prove an almost insuperable hindrance).

I have already expressed my repudiation of the teachings of 'Æstheticism'. But I must add here that I consider its fundamental standpoint legitimate and justified. It is only the *extreme* of its teaching which is obnoxious—as weak, effeminate, morbid—not its intrinsic character. I should consider 'Æstheticism' in its current significance, as the furthest extreme of the position I occupy and advocate. It seems to me that Paul Souriau's remark hits the point exactly: 'Le défaut de l'esthète, ce n'est pas de trop aimer la beauté; c'est de s'en faire une idée superficielle et étroite; de négliger les grandes beautés pour les petites.'[1] If it be objected that an attitude is bad which can lead, as it has been known to do in history, to moral turpitude, to acts of brutality and wickedness, I would answer, that for that matter there is historical evidence of men having committed similar barbarities 'ad majorem Dei gloriam', or, like Robespierre, murdered thousands out of philanthropy. Nero proves as little against the æsthetic, as these extremes against the ethical or religious standpoints.

\*     \*     \*

Let me briefly summarise the results so far obtained.

Æsthetics is the systematic study of æsthetic consciousness, of that attitude, generally called 'æsthetic', which man takes up *vis-à-vis* human life, his own experiences and the conditions of his existence in general, side by side with other equally distinctive attitudes, which may be *roughly* distinguished as practical, scientific and ethical points of view. This æsthetic consciousness finds expression and application in various forms, and Æsthetics therefore sets out to study:

[1] *La Beauté rationelle*, Paris, 1904, p. 171, fn. 1.

I. a. That form of æsthetic consciousness which is directed to, or rather results in, the creation of æsthetic objects, i.e. *artistic production:*

b. The consciousness which enjoys or contemplates works thus produced—and other objects of Nature and Reality, in so far as they are susceptible of being æsthetically contemplated, i.e. *æsthetic contemplation.*

II. The *objective* products, resulting from artistic creation, in relation to the productive and receptive consciousness, i.e. the *world of Art, fine and applied.*

III. The æsthetic consciousness extended to other spheres, and applied to Life in general, i.e. *æsthetic culture.*

\*     \*     \*

With the investigation of these fields Æsthetics may be said to have completed its task. At this point, in common with all other branches of human thought, it moves out into the Unknown and meets the great Sphinx, Metaphysics, with its fundamental problem: Why is there an æsthetic consciousness at all? What purpose does it serve, and what function does it fulfil?

It is not my intention to treat this question here, even if I were competent to do so. It is a matter for the Metaphysician rather than the Æsthetician. The answers to it are necessarily different according to the different metaphysical positions held. The materialist and idealist, the sceptic or agnostic, are as likely to disagree on this point as on any other involving metaphysical issues. All that can reasonably be expected of Æsthetics is to gather up and arrange the material that falls within its ken, and place it at the disposal of Metaphysics. It may also suggest certain conclusions which the study of æsthetic consciousness, independently of metaphysical considerations, makes possible or probable.

The *Function of Art*—to confine ourselves to this concentrated form of æsthetic consciousness—has been a matter of discussion for centuries, but there is so far little agreement about it. There is one point which I think of the highest importance for a fruitful exchange of opinion on this matter; its neglect has unnecessarily confused the issue. It is, it seems to me, essential to distinguish the *function* of Art from its *purpose*. Strictly speaking, we cannot even talk of the purpose of such a collective and, in a sense, natural phenomenon as Art. What we mean by purpose in this case is really what, in a general way, we suppose the purpose or intention of the artist or the recipient to be. The *function* of Art, on the other hand, may reveal itself in consequences independent of those consciously aimed at, in effects not intentionally striven for, but arising incidentally. The function of Art is the part played by it in the household of Nature or the Universe.

This undue identification of intention and function has done much mischief. Because the general effect of art-impressions is pleasing, it has been supposed that the intention of the recipient is to be 'pleased'. This supposition has been extended to the artist, and it has been assumed that his motive in producing work has been the wish to 'please' either himself or others. It must, of course, be admitted that this view represents an advance over older theories (still prevalent, especially in England), which maintained that the artist aimed at moral instruction or that the recipient went to theatres and museums for purposes of moral self-improvement. Yet even the more harmless view of the intention, to please and be pleased, is being gradually abandoned, thanks to a better understanding of the nature of art-production and art-effect. The realisation that in æsthetic consciousness we have to deal with a general mental attitude, a peculiar turn of mind, partly innate and partly acquired (whether by imitation, habit or spontaneous effort matters little), is leading to the growing conviction that the artist can as little help producing, or the recipient appreciating, Art, as the sun can help shining. If production and reception are thought of as sporadic acts, deliberately undertaken by some individuals, a reason will naturally be sought to explain their occurrence. But if the 'art-impulse', as a recent expression has it, is really an impulse, we can no more point to any definite purpose on the part of the individual indulging it, than we can, in terms of *intention*, say why we breathe or eat or sleep. This conception of the function of Art is corroborated by experience. The genuine artist appears to have no definitely elaborated intention in producing his work. He creates purely in conformity with his own nature, at the command of an overpowering impulse, often with an intense strain and feverish activity of all his faculties, but in ignorance of the origin or nature of his 'inspiration'. However clearly and precisely he may be able to trace the development of his conceptions, the occasions leading to them, the remoter sources enlarging them, the evolution of their concrete realisation, yet the ultimate spring of his activity is hidden by his own personality, and the 'inspiration' appears as something infinitely mysterious, undecipherable, almost divine. In a somewhat similar way, the recipient, when going to a play or a gallery, has probably no definite intention of 'being pleased'. We wish for æsthetic impressions, we decorate our houses and adorn our belongings, because we feel the instinctive need of æsthetic stimulation: 'being pleased' is merely an incidental addition to the satisfaction of our desire, as the impossibility of satisfying it is often felt as a painful deprivation. The theory of æsthetic 'pleasure' has done no little harm in robbing Art of some of its characteristic potency, making it appear to the popular mind even more superficial and shallow, by turning it into a superfluous form of 'amusement'.

The confusion of the intention of the individual with the Function of Art, and the intimate connection which necessarily exists between Art and other spheres of human experience, have inevitably led in the past to theories about its function which more or less one-sidedly emphasised its bearing upon one or other of them. Many of the metaphysical definitions of Beauty implied *ipso facto* some definite view of the function of Art as an activity which attempted to realise the absolutely Beautiful, e.g. Plato's theory of Beauty as knowledge. If we may class all doctrines of this kind—which have been transmitted in more or less mystical formulation from the late phases of antiquity to medieval scholasticism, thence through rationalism down to the present

I

time (one of its last great exponents was Taine)—as *intellectualistic* theories, we find side by side with them *moralistic* views, which enjoyed an even greater vogue. At the time of the Renaissance, when the Church was looking askance at the resuscitated paganism of Art and Literature, theorists vied with each other to find excuses for the practice of both. The general moralistic preoccupation of the times and the accusations of immorality preferred against Art only accentuated the tendency to justify its existence on moral grounds. The innumerable 'Defences of Poesy' in Italy, France and England, bear witness to the lively interest which the problem of the function of Art excited in the minds of that period. They are practically all variations on a single theme (the attempted controversion of which was the great achievement of Aristotle): that Art is the handmaid of morality, presenting either seductive examples of virtue, as in didactic art in the narrower sense, or horrifying and deterrent instances of vice, as especially in tragedy. This, in various forms and styles, was still the accepted view in the eighteenth century, represented by Shaftesbury, Lessing, Herder, Fontanelle, Voltaire, Diderot, among many others. With a distinct theological and socialistic bias it is still manifest in Ruskin and Tolstoy. A more purely *æsthetic* theory was initiated by Kant's opposition to moralistic interpretations. And despite vicissitudes, both of excess and opposition, the basic principle has survived. As I have already intimated, it seems to me unfortunate that such a fundamentally sound position as 'Art for Art's sake' should at times have been rendered uninhabitable by the intolerance and shallowness of some of its most obstinate defenders.

It is not my intention to go into details concerning these different conceptions of the function of Art. I only wish to point out that they exist. After my previous remarks, it should be obvious that any interpretation of the function and value of Art is inadequate which does not lay primary stress on the *æsthetic* aspect. But I do not wish to maintain that other aspects are unimportant, much less that they do not exist. On the contrary. The second half of the last century, by its ethnological and anthropological investigations of the part played by Art among primitive peoples, has opened up some entirely new points of view. These researches have to a large extent revolutionised our modern conception of Art as part of the scheme of human development by showing the intimate connection of primitive art-consciousness with primitive tribal life, with its religious and magical beliefs, its social institutions, its intellectual advances and material progress. Though it is inadmissible to argue straightway from the original function of a thing to its functions at later stages of evolution, the results of such investigations have powerfully contributed to the solidification and the enrichment of theories about the intellectual, moral and social function of Art. These have taken the place of the purely speculative and often nebulous conceptions of former times, and done no little to invest Art with a new interest and importance from the theoretical point of view: to reveal the fact that in Art we have to deal not with an excrescence or idle luxury of modern life, but with a real and vital force in human existence.

Nevertheless the dominant interest of Æsthetics in the function of Art is and remains its *æsthetic* function, and its æsthetic function for the *individual*. The question is not what individual effects are produced by any special work of Art upon him, but rather what are the most lasting and the most general results of his contact with Art collectively. If we say that Art makes us morally better, that it adds to our intellectual knowledge, that it exercises a beneficial socialising influence, we refer to consequences undoubtedly true and important but extra-æsthetic. The difficulty about the genuinely *æsthetic* effects is that they are so complex, their permanent consequences so unforseeable, that it is impossible to summarise them thus in a short formulation. Æsthetically speaking, we must, I think, see the function of Art, its place in the economy of the universe, as the enlargement and enrichment of our complete personality, the enhancement and quickening of our total conscious existence. The contemplative immanence of æsthetic consciousness is *par excellence* the medium for extending the limited range of our personal experience and of forcing those experiences which do fall within it into the highest relief of which they are susceptible. We cannot get away from the fact that we are all shut in within the narrow, but impenetrable walls of our own self. It is impossible for us to merge ourselves, even temporarily, into the personality even of those we know best and most intimately. However closely it may touch us, however much practical and emotional concern it may give us, the form of their experience still remains outside of ourselves and inaccessible to our direct perception. Our range of personal, actually realised experiences is deplorably small. For experiences are not communicable by intellectual knowledge *about* them, but only through our actual realisation of them. This realisation, which we as concrete individuals cannot make owing to the limitations of our sphere of action and of our practical personality, is only possible æsthetically and through the medium of Art. It is in this sense that a French writer recently coined a happy expression by defining a work of Art as 'un accumulateur de vie'. It is difficult, if not impossible, to make ourselves fully aware of the enrichment we have each of us drawn from Art. Perhaps if we look back upon childhood with its fewer, but relatively so intense, æsthetic effects, we may remember the astonished peeps into other undreamt-of worlds, through much loved books or our first pantomime, play or opera. Even in later life, when æsthetic impressions begin to crowd in upon us, a few individual works of art stand out as special revelations of new outlooks and experiences, like milestones upon the road of our development. What we are, the sum total of our most personal being, we undoubtedly owe in a much larger degree to experiences made through the medium of æsthetic impressions, than to the extension of our personality by contact with the real world. If we could subtract all the wealth bestowed upon us by Art, it is inconceivable how little would be left of what we now feel ourselves to possess. For exclusively intellectual knowledge, learning with the head about history or geography or science, however much it may widen our intellectual outlook and fit us for the assimilation of further knowledge, does not extend our *personal* horizon. Only 'æsthetic culture' educates our whole being, enriches *all* our faculties and extends our total inward life beyond the small holding which in practical life is allotted to each of us.

What, in view of this, shall we say finally about the function of Æsthetics? Its purpose I have already indicated more than once; and the immeasurable distance which separates the modern conception of its task from older speculations on the nature of the Beautiful seems to me a sufficient guarantee of the legitimacy and value of the study. But its function? Those remoter results which Æsthetics, so to speak, unconsciously and unintentionally achieves? It is a well-known fact that theoretical occupation with a subject frequently engenders a practical interest in it. Thus Æsthetics, as the abstract and scientific investigation of æsthetic consciousness and of its most pregnant form, Art, may, I think, play its part in stimulating a genuine interest in Art, and might lead to the actual realisation of what it only abstractly studies.

If this could be called its *personal* function, its bearing upon general culture might be termed its *social* function. All serious theoretical occupation with general problems implies a widening of our mental horizon and an extension of our outlook upon life. Few studies contain richer possibilities of enlarging our whole, not only our intellectual, horizon, than Æsthetics. Of it too may be said what Pater said of Philosophy: '[It] serves culture, not by the fancied gift of absolute transcendental knowledge, but by suggesting questions which help one to detect the passion, and strangeness, and dramatic contrasts of life.'

# 'Psychical Distance' as a Factor in Art and an Æsthetic Principle

I. 1. Meaning of the term 'Distance'
 2. Distance as a factor in Art
 3. Distance as an æsthetic principle

II. 1. Distance describes a personal relation
 2. The antinomy of Distance
 3. The variability of Distance
 4. Distance as the psychological formulation of the anti-realism of Art: naturalistic and idealistic Art
 5. Distance as applied to the antithesis 'sensual' and 'spiritual'
 6. Distance as applied to the antithesis 'individualistic' and 'typical'

III. Distance as an æsthetic principle:
 1. As a criterion between the agreeable and the beautiful
 2. As a phase of artistic production: falsity of the theory of 'self-expression of the artist'
 [3. Distance and some recent æsthetic theories]
 4. Distance as a fundamental principle of the 'æsthetic consciousness'

# I

1. The conception of 'Distance' suggests, in connection with Art, certain trains of thought by no means devoid of interest or of speculative importance. Perhaps the most obvious suggestion is that of *actual spatial* distance, i.e. the distance of a work of Art from the spectator, or that of *represented spatial* distance, i.e. the distance represented within the work. Less obvious, more metaphorical, is the meaning of *temporal* distance. The first was noticed already by Aristotle in his *Poetics*; the second has played a great part in the history of painting in the form of perspective; the distinction between these two kinds of distance assumes special importance theoretically in the differentiation between sculpture in the round, and relief-sculpture. Temporal distance, remoteness from us in point of time, though often a cause of misconceptions, has been declared to be a factor of considerable weight in our appreciation.

It is not, however, in any of these meanings that 'Distance' is put forward here, though it will be clear in the course of this essay that the above-mentioned kinds of distance are rather special forms of the conception of Distance as advocated here, and derive whatever *æsthetic* qualities they may possess from Distance in its *general* connotation. This general connotation is 'Psychical Distance'.

A short illustration will explain what is meant by 'Psychical Distance'. Imagine a fog at sea: for most people it is an experience of acute unpleasantness. Apart from the physical annoyance and remoter forms of discomfort such as delays, it is apt to produce feelings of peculiar anxiety, fears of invisible dangers, strains of watching and listening for distant and unlocalised signals. The listless movements of the ship and her warning calls soon tell upon the nerves of the passengers; and that special, expectant, tacit anxiety and nervousness, always associated with this experience, make a fog the dreaded terror of the sea (all the more terrifying because of its very silence and gentleness) for the expert seafarer no less than for the ignorant landsman.

Nevertheless, a fog at sea can be a source of intense relish and enjoyment. Abstract from the experience of the sea fog, for the moment, its danger and practical unpleasantness, just as every one in the enjoyment of a mountain-climb disregards its physical labour and its danger (though, it is not denied, that these may incidentally enter into the enjoyment and enhance it); direct the attention to the features 'objectively' constituting the pheno-menon—the veil surrounding you with an opaqueness as of transparent milk, blurring the outline of things and distorting their shapes into weird grotesqueness; observe the carrying-power of the air, producing the impression as if you could touch some far-off siren by merely putting out your hand and letting it lose itself behind that white wall; note the curious creamy smoothness of the water, hypocritically denying as it were any suggestion of danger; and, above all, the strange solitude and remoteness from the world, as it can be found only on the highest mountain-tops: and the experience may acquire, in its uncanny mingling of repose and terror, a flavour of such concentrated poignancy and delight as to contrast sharply with the blind and distempered anxiety of its other aspects. This contrast, often emerging with startling suddenness, is like a momentary switching on of some new current, or the passing ray of a brighter light, illuminating the out-look upon perhaps the most ordinary and familiar objects—an impression which we experience sometimes in instants of direst extremity, when our practical interest snaps like a wire from sheer over-tension, and we watch the consummation of some impending catastrophe with the marvelling unconcern of a mere spectator.

It is a difference of outlook, due—if such a metaphor is per-missible—to the insertion of Distance. This Distance appears to lie between our own self and its affections, using the latter term in its broadest sense as anything which affects our being, bodily or spiritually, e.g. as sensation, perception, emotional state or idea. Usually, though not always, it amounts to the same thing to say that the Distance lies between our own self and such objects as are the sources or vehicles of such affections.

Thus, in the fog, the transformation by Distance is produced in the first instance by putting the phenomenon, so to speak, out of gear with our practical, actual self; by allowing it to stand outside the context of our personal needs and ends—in short, by looking at it 'objectively', as it has often been called, by permitting only such reactions on our part as emphasise the 'objective' features of the experience, and by interpreting even our 'subjective' affections not as modes of *our* being but rather as characteristics of the phenomenon.

The working of Distance is, accordingly, not simple, but highly complex. It has a *negative*, inhibitory aspect—the cutting-out of the practical sides of things and of our practical attitude to them—and a *positive* side—the elaboration of the experience on the new basis created by the inhibitory action of Distance.

2. Consequently, this distanced view of things is not, and cannot be, our normal outlook. As a rule, experiences constantly turn the same side towards us, namely, that which has the strongest practical force of appeal. We are not ordinarily aware of those aspects of things which do not touch us immediately and practically, nor are we generally conscious of impressions apart from our own self which is impressed. The sudden view of things from their reverse, usually unnoticed, side, comes upon us as a revelation, and such revelations are precisely those of Art. In this most general sense, Distance is a factor in all Art.

3. It is, for this very reason, also an æsthetic principle. The æsthetic contemplation and the æsthetic outlook have often been described as 'objective'. We speak of 'objective' artists as Shakespeare or Velasquez, of 'objective' works or art-forms as Homer's *Iliad* or the drama. It is a term constantly occurring in discussions and criticisms, though its sense, if pressed at all, becomes very questionable. For certain forms of Art, such as lyrical poetry, are said to be 'subjective'; Shelley, for example, would usually be considered a 'subjective' writer. On the other hand, no work of Art can be genuinely 'objective' in the sense in which this term might be applied to a work on history or to a scientific treatise;

nor can it be 'subjective' in the ordinary acceptance of that term, as a personal feeling, a direct statement of a wish or belief, or a cry of passion is subjective. 'Objectivity' and 'subjectivity' are a pair of opposites which in their mutual exclusiveness when applied to Art soon lead to confusion.

Nor are they the only pair of opposites. Art has with equal vigour been declared alternately 'idealistic' and 'realistic', 'sensual' and 'spiritual', 'individualistic' and 'typical'. Between the defence of either terms of such antitheses most æsthetic theories have vacillated. It is one of the contentions of this essay that such opposites find their synthesis in the more fundamental conception of Distance.

Distance further provides the much needed criterion of the beautiful as distinct from the merely agreeable.

Again, it marks one of the most important steps in the process of artistic creation and serves as a distinguishing feature of what is commonly so loosely described as the 'artistic temperament'.

Finally, it may claim to be considered as one of the essential characteristics of the 'æsthetic consciousness', if I may describe by this term that special mental attitude towards, and outlook upon, experience, which finds its most pregnant expression in the various forms of Art.

## II

Distance, as I said before, is obtained by separating the object and its appeal from one's own self, by putting it out of gear with practical needs and ends. Thereby the 'contemplation' of the object becomes alone possible. But it does not mean that the relation between the self and the object is broken to the extent of becoming 'impersonal'. Of the alternatives 'personal' and 'impersonal' the latter surely comes nearer to the truth; but here, as elsewhere, we meet the difficulty of having to express certain facts in terms coined for entirely different uses. To do so usually results in paradoxes, which are nowhere more inevitable than in discussions upon Art. 'Personal' and 'impersonal', 'subjective' and 'objective' are such terms, devised for purposes other than æsthetic speculation, and becoming loose and ambiguous as soon as applied outside the sphere of their special meanings. In giving preference therefore to the term 'impersonal' to describe the relation between the spectator and a work of Art, it is to be noticed that it is not impersonal in the sense in which we speak of the 'impersonal' character of Science, for instance. In order to obtain 'objectively valid' results, the scientist excludes the 'personal factor', i.e. his personal wishes as to the validity of his results, his predilection for any particular system to be proved or disproved by his research. It goes without saying that all experiments and investigations are undertaken out of a personal interest in the science, for the ultimate support of a definite assumption, and involve personal hopes of success; but this does not affect the 'dispassionate' attitude of the investigator, under pain of being accused of 'manufacturing his evidence'.

1. Distance does not imply an impersonal, purely intellectually interested relation of such a kind. On the contrary, it describes a *personal* relation, often highly emotionally coloured, but *of a peculiar character*. Its peculiarity lies in that the personal character of the relation has been, so to speak, filtered. It has been cleared of the practical, concrete nature of its appeal, without, however, thereby losing its original constitution. One of the best-known examples is to be found in our attitude towards the events and characters of the drama: they appeal to us like persons and incidents of normal experience, except that that side of their appeal, which would usually affect us in a directly personal manner, is held in abeyance. This difference, so well known as to be almost trivial, is generally explained by reference to the knowledge that the characters and situations are 'unreal', imaginary. In this sense Witasek[1] operating with Meinong's theory of *Annahmen*, has described the emotions involved in witnessing a drama as

[1] H. Witasek, 'Zur psychologischen Analyse der æsthetischen Einfühlung', *Ztsch. f. Psychol. u. Physiol. der Sinnesorg.*, 1901, xxv, 1 ff.; *Grundzüge der Æsthetik*, Leipzig, 1904.

*Scheingefühle*, a term which has so frequently been misunderstood in discussions of his theories. But, as a matter of fact, the 'assumption' upon which the imaginative emotional reaction is based is not necessarily the condition, but often the consequence, of Distance; that is to say, the converse of the reason usually stated would then be true: viz. that Distance, by changing our relation to the characters, renders them seemingly fictitious, not that the fictitiousness of the characters alters our feelings toward them. It is, of course, to be granted that the actual and admitted unreality of the dramatic action reinforces the effect of Distance. But surely the proverbial unsophisticated yokel, whose chivalrous interference in the play on behalf of the hapless heroine can only be prevented by impressing upon him that 'they are only pretending', is not the ideal type of theatrical audience. The proof of the seeming paradox that it is Distance which primarily gives to dramatic action the appearance of unreality and not vice versa, is the observation that the same filtration of our sentiments and the same seeming 'unreality' of *actual* men and things occur, when at times, by a sudden change of inward perspective, we are overcome by the feeling that 'all the world's a stage'.

2. This personal, but 'distanced' relation (as I will venture to call this nameless character of our view) directs attention to a strange fact which appears to be one of the fundamental paradoxes of Art: it is what I propose to call 'the antinomy of Distance'.

It will be readily admitted that a work of Art has the more chance of appealing to us the better it finds us prepared for its particular kind of appeal. Indeed, without some degree of predisposition on our part, it must necessarily remain incomprehensible, and to that extent unappreciated. The success and intensity of its appeal would seem, therefore, to stand in direct proportion to the completeness with which it corresponds with our intellectual and emotional peculiarities and the idiosyncrasies of our experience. The absence of such a concordance between the characters of a work and of the spectator is, of course, the most general explanation for differences of 'tastes'.

At the same time, such a principle of concordance requires a qualification, which leads at once to the antinomy of Distance.

Suppose a man, who believes that he has cause to be jealous about his wife, witnesses a performance of *Othello*. He will the more perfectly appreciate the situation, conduct and character of Othello, the more exactly the feelings and experiences of Othello coincide with his own—at least he *ought* to on the above principle of concordance. In point of fact, he will probably do anything but appreciate the play. In reality, the concordance will merely render him acutely conscious of his own jealousy; by a sudden reversal of perspective he will no longer see Othello apparently betrayed by Desdemona, but himself in an analogous situation with his own wife. This reversal of perspective is the consequence of the loss of Distance.

If this be taken as a typical case, it follows that the qualification required is that the coincidence should be as complete as is compatible with maintaining Distance. The jealous spectator of *Othello* will indeed appreciate and enter into the play the more keenly, the greater the resemblance with his own experience— *provided* that he succeeds in keeping the Distance between the action of the play and his personal feelings: a very difficult performance in the circumstances. It is on account of the same difficulty that the expert and the professional critic make a bad audience, since their expertness and critical professionalism are *practical* activities, involving their concrete personality and constantly endangering their Distance. [It is, by the way, one of the reasons why Criticism is an art, for it requires the constant interchange from the practical to the distanced attitude and vice versa, which is characteristic of artists.]

The same qualification applies to the artist. He will prove artistically most effective in the formulation of an intensely *personal* experience, but he can formulate it artistically only on condition of a detachment from the experience *qua personal*. Hence the statement of so many artists that artistic formulation was to them a kind of catharsis, a means of ridding themselves of feelings and ideas the acuteness of which they felt almost as a kind of obsession. Hence, on the other hand, the failure of the average man to convey to others at all adequately the impression of an overwhelming joy or sorrow. His personal implication in the event renders it impossible for him to formulate and present it in such a way as to make others, like himself, feel all the meaning and fullness which it possesses for him.

What is therefore, both in appreciation and production, most desirable is the *utmost decrease of Distance without its disappearance*.

3. Closely related, in fact a presupposition to the 'antinomy', is the *variability* of Distance. Herein especially lies the advantage of Distance compared with such terms as 'objectivity' and 'detachment'. Neither of them implies a *personal* relation—indeed both actually preclude it; and the mere inflexibility and exclusiveness of their opposites render their application generally meaningless.

Distance, on the contrary, admits naturally of degrees, and differs not only according to the nature of the *object*, which may impose a greater or smaller degree of Distance, but varies also according to the *individual's capacity* for maintaining a greater or lesser degree. And here one may remark that not only do *persons differ from each other* in their habitual measure of Distance, but that the *same individual differs* in his ability to maintain it in the face of different objects and of different arts.

There exist, therefore, two different sets of conditions affecting the degree of Distance in any given case: those offered by the object and those realised by the subject. In their interplay they afford one of the most extensive explanations for varieties of æsthetic experience, since loss of Distance, whether due to the one or the other, means loss of æsthetic appreciation.

In short, Distance may be said *to be variable both according to the distancing-power of the individual, and according to the character of the object*.

There are two ways of losing Distance: either to 'under-distance' or to 'over-distance'. 'Under-distancing' is the commonest failing of the *subject*, an excess of Distance is a frequent failing of *Art*, especially in the past. Historically it looks almost as if Art had attempted to meet the deficiency of Distance on the part of the subject and had overshot the mark in this endeavour. It will be seen later that this is actually true, for it appears that over-distanced Art is specially designed for a class of appreciation which has difficulty to rise spontaneously to any degree of Distance. The consequence of a loss of Distance through one or other cause is familiar: the verdict in the case of under-distancing is that the work is 'crudely naturalistic', 'harrowing', 'repulsive in its realism'. An excess of Distance produces the impression of improbability, artificiality, emptiness or absurdity.

The individual tends, as I just stated, to under-distance rather than to lose Distance by over-distancing. *Theoretically* there is no limit to the decrease of Distance. In theory, therefore, not only the usual subjects of Art, but even the most personal affections, whether ideas, percepts or emotions, can be sufficiently distanced to be æsthetically appreciable. Especially artists are gifted in this direction to a remarkable extent. The average individual, on the contrary, very rapidly reaches his limit of decreasing Distance, his 'Distance-limit', i.e. that point at which Distance is lost and appreciation either disappears or changes its character.

In the *practice*, therefore, of the average person, a limit does exist which marks the minimum at which his appreciation can maintain itself in the æsthetic field, and this average minimum lies considerably higher than the Distance-limit of the artist. It is practically impossible to fix this average limit, in the absence of data, and on account of the wide fluctuations from person to person to which this limit is subject. But it is safe to infer that, in art practice, explicit references to organic affections, to the material existence of the body, especially to sexual matters, lie normally below the Distance-limit, and can be touched upon by Art only with special precautions. Allusions to social institutions of any degree of personal importance—in particular, allusions implying any doubt as to their validity—the questioning of some generally recognised ethical sanctions, references to topical subjects occupying public attention at the moment, and such like, are all danger-ously near the average limit and may at any time fall below it, arousing, instead of æsthetic appreciation, concrete hostility or mere amusement.

This difference in the Distance-limit between artists and the public has been the source of much misunderstanding and in-justice. Many an artist has seen his work condemned and himself ostracised for the sake of so-called 'immoralities' which to him were bona fide æsthetic objects. His power of distancing, nay, the necessity of distancing feelings, sensations, situations which for the average person are too intimately bound up with his concrete existence to be regarded in that light, have often quite unjustly earned for him accusations of cynicism, sensualism, morbidness or frivolity. The same misconception has arisen over many 'problem plays' and 'problem novels' in which the public have persisted in seeing nothing but a supposed 'problem' of the moment, whereas the author may have been—and often has demonstrably been—able to distance the subject-matter sufficiently to rise above its practical problematic import and to regard it simply as a dramatic-ally and humanly interesting situation.

The variability of Distance in respect to Art, disregarding for the moment the subjective complication, appears both as a general feature in Art, and in the differences between the special arts.

It has been an old problem why the 'arts of the eye and of the ear' should have reached the practically exclusive predominance over arts of other senses. Attempts to raise 'culinary art' to the level of a Fine Art have failed in spite of all propaganda, as com-pletely as the creation of scent or liqueur 'symphonies'. There is little doubt that, apart from other excellent reasons[1] of a partly psycho-physical, partly technical nature, the actual, *spatial distance* separating objects of sight and hearing from the subject has con-tributed strongly to the development of this monopoly. In a

[1] J. Volkelt, 'Die Bedeutung der niederen Empfindungen für die æsthetische Einfühlung', *Ztsch. f. Psychol. u. Physiol. der Sinnesorg.*, xxxii, 15, 16; *System der Æsthetik*, 1905, 1, 260 ff.

similar manner *temporal remoteness* produces Distance, and objects removed from us in point of time are *ipso facto* distanced to an extent which was impossible for their contemporaries. Many pictures, plays and poems had, as a matter of fact, rather an expository or illustrative significance—as for instance much ecclesiastical Art—or the force of a direct practical appeal—as the invectives of many satires or comedies—which seem to us nowadays irreconcilable with their æsthetic claims. Such works have consequently profited greatly by lapse of time and have reached the level of Art only with the help of temporal distance, while others, on the contrary, often for the same reason have suffered a loss of Distance, through *over*-distancing.

Special mention must be made of a group of artistic conceptions which present excessive Distance in their form of appeal rather than in their actual presentation—a point illustrating the necessity of distinguishing between distancing an object and distancing the appeal of which it is the source. I mean here what is often rather loosely termed 'idealistic Art', that is, Art springing from abstract conceptions, expressing allegorical meanings, or illustrating general truths. Generalisations and abstractions suffer under this disadvantage that they have too much general applicability to invite a personal interest in them, and too little individual concreteness to prevent them applying to us in all their force. They appeal to everybody and therefore to none. An axiom of Euclid belongs to nobody, just because it compels everyone's assent; general conceptions like Patriotism, Friendship, Love, Hope, Life, Death, concern as much Dick, Tom and Harry as myself, and I, therefore, either feel unable to get into any kind of personal relation to them, or, if I do so, they become at once, emphatically and concretely, *my* Patriotism, *my* Friendship, *my* Love, *my* Hope, *my* Life and Death. By mere force of generalisation, a general truth or a universal ideal is so far distanced from myself that I fail to realise it concretely at all, or, when I do so, I can realise it only as part of my *practical actual being*, i.e. it falls below the Distance-limit altogether. 'Idealistic Art' suffers consequently under the

peculiar difficulty that its excess of Distance turns generally into
an *under*-distanced appeal—all the more easily, as it is the usual
failing of the subject to *under*—rather than to *over*-distance.

The different special arts show at the present time very marked
variations in the degree of Distance which they usually impose
or require for their appreciation. Unfortunately here again the
absence of data makes itself felt and indicates the necessity of con-
ducting observations, possibly experiments, so as to place these
suggestions upon a securer basis. In one single art, viz. the *theatre*,
a small amount of information is available, from an unexpected
source, namely the proceedings of the censorship committee,[1]
which on closer examination might be made to yield evidence of
interest to the psychologist. In fact, the whole censorship problem,
as far as it does not turn upon purely economic questions, may be
said to hinge upon Distance; if every member of the public could
be trusted to keep it, there would be no sense whatever in the
existence of a censor of plays. There is, of course, no doubt that,
speaking generally, theatrical performances *eo ipso* run a special
risk of a loss of Distance owing to the material presentment[2] of its
subject-matter. The physical presence of living human beings as
vehicles of dramatic art is a difficulty which no art has to face in the
same way. A similar, in many ways even greater, risk confronts
*dancing*: though attracting perhaps a less widely spread human
interest, its animal spirits are frequently quite unrelieved by any
glimmer of spirituality and consequently form a proportionately
stronger lure to under-distancing. In the higher forms of dancing
technical execution of the most wearing kind makes up a great
deal for its intrinsic tendency towards a loss of Distance, and as a
popular performance, at least in southern Europe, it has retained
much of its ancient artistic glamour, producing a peculiarly subtle
balancing of Distance between the pure delight of bodily move-

[1] Report from the Joint Select Committee of the House of Lords and the House
of Commons on Stage Plays (Censorship), 1909.

[2] I shall use the term 'presentment' to denote the manner of presenting, in
distinction to 'presentation' as that which is presented.

ment and high technical accomplishment. In passing, it is interesting to observe (as bearing upon the development of Distance)
that this art, once as much a fine art as music and considered by the
Greeks as a particularly valuable educational exercise, should—
except in sporadic cases—have fallen so low from the pedestal it
once occupied. Next to the theatre and dancing stands *sculpture*.
Though not using a *living* bodily medium, yet the human form in
its full spatial materiality constitutes a similar threat to Distance.
Our northern habits of dress and ignorance of the human body
have enormously increased the difficulty of distancing Sculpture,
in part through the gross misconceptions to which it is exposed, in
part owing to a complete lack of standards of bodily perfection,
and an inability to realise the distinction between sculptural form
and bodily shape, which is the only but fundamental point distinguishing a statue from a cast taken from life. In *painting* it is
apparently the form of its presentment and the usual reduction in
scale which would explain why this art can venture to approach
more closely than sculpture to the normal Distance-limit. As this
matter will be discussed later in a special connection this simple
reference may suffice here. *Music* and *architecture* have a curious
position. These two most abstract of all arts show a remarkable
fluctuation in their Distances. Certain kinds of music, especially
'pure' music, or 'classical' or 'heavy' music, appear for many
people over-distanced; light, 'catchy' tunes, on the contrary, easily
reach that degree of decreasing Distance below which they cease
to be Art and become a pure amusement. In spite of its strange
abstractness which to many philosophers has made it comparable
to architecture and mathematics, music possesses a sensuous,
frequently sensual, character: the undoubted physiological and
muscular stimulus of its melodies and harmonies, no less than its
rhythmic aspects, would seem to account for the occasional disappearance of Distance. To this might be added its strong tendency, especially in unmusical people, to stimulate trains of
thought quite disconnected with itself, following channels of
subjective inclinations—day-dreams of a more or less directly

personal character. *Architecture* requires almost uniformly a very great Distance; that is to say, the majority of persons derive no æsthetic appreciation from architecture as such, apart from the incidental impression of its decorative features and its associations. The causes are numerous, but prominent among them are the confusion of building with architecture and the predominance of utilitarian purposes, which overshadow the architectural claims upon the attention.

4. That all art requires a Distance-limit beyond which, and a Distance within which only, æsthetic appreciation becomes possible, is the *psychological formulation of a general characteristic of Art*, viz. its *anti-realistic nature*. Though seemingly paradoxical, this applies as much to 'naturalistic' as to 'idealistic' Art. The difference commonly expressed by these epithets is at bottom merely the difference in the degree of Distance; and this produces, so far as 'naturalism' and 'idealism' in Art are not meaningless labels, the usual result that what appears obnoxiously 'naturalistic' to one person, may be 'idealistic' to another. To say that Art is anti-realistic simply insists upon the fact that Art is not nature, never pretends to be nature and strongly resists any confusion with nature. It emphasises the *art*-character of Art: 'artistic' is synonymous with 'anti-realistic'; it explains even sometimes a very marked degree of artificiality.

'Art is an imitation of nature', was the current art-conception in the eighteenth century. It is the fundamental axiom of the standard work of that time upon æsthetic theory by the Abbé Du Bos, *Réflexions critiques sur la poésie et la peinture*, 1719; the idea received strong support from the literal acceptance of Aristotle's theory of μίμησις and produced echoes everywhere, in Lessing's *Laokoon* no less than in Burke's famous statement that 'all Art is great as it deceives'. Though it may be assumed that since the time of Kant and of the Romanticists this notion has died out, it still lives in unsophisticated minds. Even when formally denied, it persists, for instance, in the belief that 'Art idealises nature', which means after all only that Art copies nature with certain improvements and revisions. Artists themselves are unfortunately often responsible for the spreading of this conception. Whistler indeed said that to produce Art by imitating nature would be like trying to produce music by sitting upon the piano, but the selective, idealising imitation of nature finds merely another support in such a saying. Naturalism, pleinairism, impressionism, even the guileless enthusiasm of the artist for the works of nature, her wealth of suggestion, her delicacy of workmanship, for the steadfastness of her guidance, only produce upon the public the impression that Art is, after all, an imitation of nature. Then how can it be anti-realistic? The antithesis, Art *versus* nature, seems to break down. Yet if it does, what is the sense of Art?

Here the conception of Distance comes to the rescue. The solution of the dilemma lies in the 'antinomy of Distance' with its demand: utmost decrease of Distance without its disappearance. The simple observation that Art is the more effective, the more it falls into line with our predispositions which are inevitably moulded on general experience and nature, has always been the original motive for 'naturalism'. 'Naturalism', 'impressionism' is no new thing; it is only a new name for an innate leaning of Art, from the time of the Chaldeans and Egyptians down to the present day. Even the Apollo of Tenea apparently struck his contemporaries as so startlingly 'naturalistic' that the subsequent legend attributed a superhuman genius to his creator. A constantly closer approach to nature, a perpetual refining of the limit of Distance, yet without overstepping the dividing line of art and nature, has always been the inborn bent of art. To deny this dividing line has occasionally been the failing of naturalism. But no theory of naturalism is complete which does not at the same time allow for the intrinsic idealism of Art: for both are merely degrees in that wide range lying beyond the Distance-limit. To imitate nature so as to trick the spectator into the deception that it is nature which he beholds, is to forsake Art, its anti-realism, its distanced spirituality, and to fall below the limit into sham, sensationalism or platitude.

But what, in the theory of antinomy of Distance, requires explanation is the existence of an *idealistic, highly distanced* Art. There are numerous reasons to account for it; indeed in so complex a phenomenon as Art, *single* causes can be pronounced almost *a priori* to be false. Foremost among such causes which have contributed to the formation of an idealistic Art appears to stand the subordination of Art to some extraneous purpose of an impressive, exceptional character. Such a subordination has consisted—at various epochs of Art history—in the use to which Art was put to subserve commemorative, hieratic, generally religious, royal or patriotic functions. The object to be commemorated had to stand out from among other still existing objects or persons; the thing or the being to be worshipped had to be distinguished as markedly as possible from profaner objects of reverence and had to be invested with an air of sanctity by a removal from its ordinary context of occurrence. Nothing could have assisted more powerfully the introduction of a high Distance than this attempt to differentiate objects of common experience in order to fit them for their exalted position. Curious, unusual things of nature met this tendency half-way and easily assumed divine rank; but others had to be distanced by an exaggeration of their size, by extraordinary attributes, by strange combinations of human and animal forms, by special insistence upon particular characteristics, or by the careful removal of all noticeably individualistic and concrete features. Nothing could be more striking than the contrast, for example, in Egyptian Art between the monumental, stereotyped effigies of the Pharaohs, and the startlingly realistic rendering of domestic scenes and of ordinary mortals, such as 'the Scribe' or 'the Village Sheikh'. Equally noteworthy is the exceeding artificiality of Russian eikon-painting with its prescribed attributes, expressions and gestures. Even Greek dramatic practice appears to have aimed, for similar purposes and in marked contrast to our stage-habits, at an increase rather than at a decrease of Distance. Otherwise Greek Art, even of a religious type, is remarkable for its *low* Distance value; and it speaks highly for the æsthetic capacities of the Greeks that the degree of realism which they ventured to impart to the representations of their gods, while humanising them, did not, at least at first,[1] impair the reverence of their feelings towards them. But apart from such special causes, idealistic Art of great Distance has appeared at intervals, for apparently no other reason than that the great Distance was felt to be essential to its *art*-character. What is noteworthy and runs counter to many accepted ideas is that such periods were usually epochs of a low level of general culture. These were times, which, like childhood, required the marvellous, the extraordinary, to satisfy their artistic longings, and neither realised nor cared for the poetic or artistic qualities of ordinary things. They were frequently times in which the mass of the people were plunged in ignorance and buried under a load of misery, and in which even the small educated class sought rather amusement or a pastime in Art; or they were epochs of a strong practical common sense too much concerned with the rough-and-tumble of life to have any sense of its æsthetic charms. Art was to them what melodrama is to a sec-tion of the public at the present time, and its wide Distance was the safeguard of its artistic character. The flowering periods of Art have, on the contrary, always borne the evidence of a narrow Distance. Greek Art, as just mentioned, was realistic to an extent which we, spoilt as we are by modern developments, can grasp with difficulty, but which the contrast with its oriental contem-poraries sufficiently proves. During the Augustan period—which Art historians at last are coming to regard no longer as merely 'degenerated' Greek Art—Roman Art achieved its greatest triumphs in an almost naturalistic portrait-sculpture. In the Renaissance we need only think of the realism of portraiture, sometimes amounting almost to cynicism, of the *désinvolture* with which the mistresses of popes and dukes were posed as madonnas, saints and goddesses apparently without any detriment to the

---

[1] That this practice did, in course of time, undermine their religious faith, is clear from the plays of Euripides and from Plato's condemnation of Homer's mythology.

æsthetic appeal of the works, and of the remarkable interpenetration of Art with the most ordinary routine of life, in order to realise the scarcely perceptible dividing line between the sphere of Art and the realm of practical existence. In a sense, the assertion that idealistic Art marks periods of a generally low and narrowly restricted culture is the converse to the oft-repeated statement that the flowering periods of Art coincide with epochs of decadence: for this so-called decadence represents indeed in certain respects a process of disintegration, politically, racially, often nationally, but a disruption necessary to the formation of larger social units and to the breakdown of outgrown national restrictions. For this very reason it has usually also been the sign of the growth of personal independence and of an expansion of individual culture.

To proceed to some more special points illustrating the distanced and therefore anti-realistic character of art: both in subject-matter and in the form of presentation Art has always safeguarded its distanced view. Fanciful, even fantastic, subjects have from time immemorial been the accredited material of Art. No doubt things, as well as our view of them, have changed in the course of time: *Polyphemus* and the *Lotus-Eaters* for the Greeks, the *Venusberg* or the *Magnetic Mountain* for the Middle Ages were less incredible, more realistic than to us. But *Peter Pan* or *L'Oiseau Bleu* still appeal at the present day in spite of the prevailing note of realism of our time. 'Probability' and 'improbability' in Art are not to be measured by their correspondence (or lack of it) with actual experience. To do so had involved the theories of the fifteenth to the eighteenth centuries in endless contradictions. It is rather a matter of *consistency* of Distance. The note of realism, set by a work as a whole, determines *intrinsically* the greater or smaller degree of fancy which it permits; and consequently we feel the loss of Peter Pan's shadow to be infinitely more probable than some trifling improbability which shocks our sense of proportion in a naturalistic work. No doubt also, fairy-tales, fairy-plays, stories of strange adventures were primarily invented to satisfy the craving of curiosity, the desire for the marvellous, the shudder of the unwonted and the longing for imaginary experiences. But by their mere eccentricity in regard to the normal facts of experience they cannot have failed to arouse a strong feeling of Distance.

Again, certain conventional subjects taken from mythical and legendary traditions, at first closely connected with the concrete, practical, life of a devout public, have gradually, by the mere force of convention as much as by their inherent anti-realism, acquired Distance for us today. Our view of Greek mythological sculpture, of early Christian saints and martyrs must be considerably distanced, compared with that of the Greek and medieval worshipper. It is in part the result of lapse of time, but in part also a real change of attitude. Already the outlook of the Imperial Roman had altered, and Pausanias shows a curious dualism of standpoint, declaring the Athene Lemnia to be the supreme achievement of Phidias's genius, and gazing awe-struck upon the roughly hewn tree-trunk representing some primitive Apollo. Our understanding of Greek tragedy suffers admittedly under our inability to revert to the point of view for which it was originally written. Even the tragedies of Racine demand an imaginative effort to put ourselves back into the courtly atmosphere of red-heeled, powdered ceremony. Provided the Distance is not too wide, the result of its intervention has everywhere been to enhance the *art*-character of such works and to lower their original ethical and social force of appeal. Thus in the central dome of the Church (Sta Maria dei Miracoli) at Saronno are depicted the heavenly hosts in ascending tiers, crowned by the benevolent figure of the Divine Father, bending from the window of heaven to bestow His blessing upon the assembled community. The mere realism of foreshortening and of the boldest vertical perspective may well have made the naïve Christian of the sixteenth century conscious of the Divine Presence—but for us it has become a work of Art.

The unusual, exceptional, has found its especial home in tragedy. It has always—except in highly distanced tragedy—been a popular objection to it that 'there is enough sadness in life without going to the theatre for it'. Already Aristotle appears to have met with this view among his contemporaries clamouring for 'happy endings'. Yet tragedy is not sad; if it were, there would indeed be little sense in its existence. For the tragic is just in so far different from the merely sad, as it is distanced; and it is largely the exceptional which produces the Distance of tragedy: exceptional situations, exceptional characters, exceptional destinies and conduct. Not of course characters merely cranky, eccentric, pathological. The exceptional element in tragic figures—that which makes them so utterly different from characters we meet with in ordinary experience—is a consistency of direction, a fervour of ideality, a persistence and driving-force which is far above the capacities of average men. The tragic of tragedy would, transposed into ordinary life, in nine cases out of ten, end in drama, in comedy, even in farce, for lack of steadfastness, for fear of conventions, for the dread of 'scenes', for a hundred-and-one petty faithlessnesses towards a belief or an ideal: even if for none of these, it would end in a compromise simply because man forgets and time heals.[1] Again, the sympathy which aches with the sadness of tragedy is another such confusion, the under-distancing of tragedy's appeal. Tragedy trembles always on the knife-edge of a *personal* reaction, and sympathy which finds relief in tears tends almost always towards a loss of Distance. Such a loss naturally renders tragedy unpleasant to a degree: it becomes sad, dismal, harrowing, depressing. But real tragedy (melodrama has a very strong tendency to speculate upon sympathy), truly appreciated, is not sad.

[1] The famous 'unity of time', so senseless as a 'canon', is all the same often an indispensable condition of tragedy. For in many a tragedy the catastrophe would be even intrinsically impossible, if fatality did not overtake the hero with that rush which gives no time to forget and none to heal. It is in cases such as these that criticism has often blamed the work for 'improbability'—the old confusion between Art and nature—forgetting that the death of the hero is the convention of the art-form, as much as grouping in a picture is such a convention and that probability is not the correspondence with average experience, but consistency of Distance.

'The pity of it—oh, the pity of it', that essence of all genuine tragedy is not the pity of mild, regretful sympathy. It is a chaos of tearless, bitter bewilderment, of upsurging revolt and rapturous awe before the ruthless and inscrutable fate; it is the homage to the great and exceptional in the man who in a last effort of spiritual tension can rise to confront blind, crowning Necessity even in his crushing defeat.

As I explained earlier, the form of presentation sometimes endangers the maintenance of Distance, but it more frequently acts as a considerable support. Thus the bodily vehicle of *drama* is the chief factor of risk to Distance. But, as if to counterbalance a confusion with nature, other features of stage-presentation exercise an opposite influence. Such are the general theatrical *milieu*, the shape and arrangement of the stage, the artificial lighting, the costumes, *mise en scène* and make-up, even the language, especially verse. Modern reforms of staging, aiming primarily at the removal of artistic incongruities between excessive decoration and the living figures of the actors and at the production of a more homogeneous stage-picture, inevitably work also towards a greater emphasis and homogeneity of Distance. The history of staging and dramaturgy is closely bound up with the evolution of Distance, and its fluctuations lie at the bottom not only of the greater part of all the talk and writing about 'dramatic probability' and the Aristotelian 'unities', but also of 'theatrical illusion'. In *sculpture*, one distancing factor of presentment is its lack of colour. The æsthetic, or rather inæsthetic, effect of realistic colouring is in no way touched by the controversial question of its use historically; its attempted resuscitation, such as by Klinger, seems only to confirm its disadvantages. The distancing use even of pedestals, although originally no doubt serving other purposes, is evident to anyone who has experienced the oppressively crowded sensation of moving in a room among life-sized statues placed directly upon the floor. The circumstance that the space of statuary is the same space as ours (in distinction to relief sculpture or painting, for instance) renders a distancing by pedestals, i.e. a removal from our spatial context, imperative.[1] Probably the framing of *pictures* might be shown to serve a similar purpose—though paintings have intrinsically a much greater Distance—because neither their space (perspective and imaginary space) nor their lighting coincides with our (actual) space or light, and the usual reduction in scale of the represented objects prevents a feeling of undue proximity. Besides, painting always retains to some extent a *two-*dimensional character, and this character supplies *eo ipso* a Distance. Nevertheless, life-size pictures, especially if they possess strong relief, and their light happens to coincide with the actual lighting, can occasionally produce the impression of actual presence which is a far from pleasant, though fortunately only a passing, illusion. For decorative purposes, in pictorial renderings of vistas, garden-perspectives and architectural extensions, the removal of Distance has often been consciously striven after, whether with æsthetically satisfactory results is much disputed.

A general help towards Distance (and therewith an anti-realistic feature) is to be found in the 'unification of presentment'[2] of all art-objects. By unification of presentment are meant such qualities as symmetry, opposition, proportion, balance, rhythmical distribution of parts, light-arrangements, in fact all so-called 'formal' features, 'composition' in the widest sense. Unquestionably, Distance is not the only, nor even the principal function of composition; it serves to render our grasp of the presentation easier and to increase its intelligibility. It may even in itself constitute the principal æsthetic feature of the object, as in linear complexes or patterns, partly also in architectural designs. Yet, its distancing effect can hardly be underrated. For, every kind of visibly intentional arrangement or unification must, by the mere fact of its presence, enforce Distance, by distinguishing the object

---

[1] An instance which might be adduced to disprove this point only shows its correctness on closer inspection: for it was on purpose and with the intention of removing Distance, that Rodin originally intended his *citoyens de Calais* to be placed, without pedestals, upon the market-place of that town.

[2] See note 2, p. 104.

from the confused, disjointed and scattered forms of actual experience. This function can be gauged in a typical form in cases
where composition produces an exceptionally marked impression
of artificiality (not in the bad sense of that term, but in the sense in
which all art is artificial); and it is a natural corollary to the differences of Distance in different arts and of different subjects, that the
arts and subjects vary in the degree of artificiality which they can
bear. It is this sense of artificial finish which is the source of so
much of that elaborate charm of Byzantine work, of Moham-
medan decoration, of the hieratic stiffness of so many primitive
madonnas and saints. In general the emphasis of composition and
technical finish increases with the Distance of the subject-matter:
heroic conceptions lend themselves better to verse than to prose;
monumental statues require a more general treatment, more
elaboration of setting and artificiality of pose than impressionistic
statuettes like those of Troubetzkoi; an ecclesiastic subject is
painted with a degree of symmetrical arrangement which would
be ridiculous in a Dutch interior, and a naturalistic drama carefully avoids the tableau impression characteristic of a mystery
play. In a similar manner the variations of Distance in the arts go
hand in hand with a visibly greater predominance of composition
and 'formal' elements, reaching a climax in architecture and
music. It is again a matter of 'consistency of Distance'. At the same
time, while from the point of view of the artist this is undoubtedly
the case, from the point of view of the public the emphasis of
composition and technical finish appears frequently to relieve the
impression of highly distanced subjects by *diminishing the Distance
of the whole*. The spectator has a tendency to see in composition
and finish merely evidence of the artist's 'cleverness', of his
mastery over his material. Manual dexterity is an enviable thing
to possess in everyone's experience, and naturally appeals to the
public *practically*, thereby putting it into a directly personal relation to things which intrinsically have very little personal appeal
for it. It is true that this function of composition is hardly an
æsthetic one: for the admiration of mere technical cleverness is not

an artistic enjoyment, but by a fortunate chance it has saved from oblivion and entire loss, among much rubbish, also much genuine Art, which otherwise would have completely lost contact with our life.

5. This discussion, necessarily sketchy and incomplete, may have helped to illustrate the sense in which, I suggested, Distance appears as a fundamental principle to which such antitheses as idealism and realism are reducible. The difference between 'idealistic' and 'realistic' Art is not a clear-cut dividing-line between the art-practices described by these terms, but is a difference of degree in the Distance-limit which they presuppose on the part both of the artist and of the public. A similar reconciliation seems to me possible between the opposites 'sensual' and 'spiritual', 'individual' and 'typical'. That the appeal of Art is sensuous, even sensual, must be taken as an indisputable fact. Puritanism will never be persuaded, and rightly so, that this is not the case. The sensuousness of Art is a natural implication of the 'antinomy of Distance', and will appear again in another connection. The point of importance here is that the whole sensual side of Art is purified, spiritualised, 'filtered' as I expressed it earlier, by Distance. The most sensual appeal becomes the translucent veil of an underlying spirituality, once the grossly personal and practical elements have been removed from it. And—a matter of special emphasis here—*this spiritual aspect of the appeal is the more penetrating, the more personal and direct its sensual appeal would have been* BUT FOR THE PRESENCE OF DISTANCE. For the artist, to trust in this delicate transmutation is a natural act of faith which the Puritan hesitates to venture upon: which of the two, one asks, is the greater idealist?

6. The same argument applies to the contradictory epithets 'individual' and 'typical'. A discussion in support of the fundamental individualism of Art lies outside the scope of this essay. Every artist has taken it for granted. Besides it is rather in the sense of 'concrete' or 'individualised', that it is usually opposed to 'typical'. On the other hand, 'typical', in the sense of 'abstract', is

as diametrically opposed to the whole nature of Art, as individualism is characteristic of it. It is in the sense of 'generalised' as a
'general human element' that it is claimed as a necessary in-
gredient in Art. This antithesis is again one which naturally and
without mutual sacrifice finds room within the conception of
Distance. Historically the 'typical' has had the effect of counter-
acting *under*-distancing as much as the 'individual' has opposed
*over*-distancing. Naturally the two ingredients have constantly
varied in the history of Art; they represent, in fact, two sets of
conditions to which Art has invariably been subject: the personal
and the social factors. It is Distance which on one side prevents the
emptying of Art of its concreteness and the development of the
typical into abstractness; which, on the other, suppresses the
directly personal element of its individualism; thus reducing the
antitheses to the peaceful interplay of these two factors. It is just
this interplay which constitutes the 'antinomy of Distance'.

### III

It remains to indicate the value of Distance as *an æsthetic principle*: as criterion in some of the standing problems of Æsthetics;
as representing a phase of artistic creation; and as a characteristic
feature of the 'æsthetic consciousness'.

 1. The axiom of 'hedonistic Æsthetics' is that beauty is pleasure.
Unfortunately for hedonism the formula is not reversible: not all
pleasure is beauty. Hence the necessity of some limiting criterion
to separate the beautiful within the 'pleasure-field' from the
merely agreeable. This relation of the beautiful to the agreeable is
the ever-recurring crux of all hedonistic Æsthetics, as the problem
of this relation becomes inevitable when once the hedonistic basis
is granted. It has provoked a number of widely different solutions,
some manifestly wrong, and all as little satisfactory as the whole
hedonistic groundwork upon which they rest: the shareableness
of beauty as opposed to the 'monopoly' of the agreeable (Bain),[1]

---

[1] Bain, *The Emotions and the Will*, 2nd ed., 1850.

the passivity of beauty-pleasure (Grant Allen)[1] or most recently, the 'relative permanence of beauty-pleasure in revival' (H. R. Marshall).[2]

Distance offers a distinction which is as simple in its operation as it is fundamental in its importance: *the agreeable is a non-distanced pleasure*. Beauty in the widest sense of æsthetic value is impossible without the insertion of Distance. The agreeable stands in precisely the same relation to the beautiful (in its narrower sense) as the sad stands to the tragic, as indicated earlier. Translating the above formula, one may say that the agreeable is felt as an affection of our concrete, practical self; the centre of gravity of an agreeable experience lies in the self which experiences the agreeable. The æsthetic experience, on the contrary, has its centre of gravity in itself or in the object mediating it, not in the self which has been distanced out of the field of the inner vision of the experiencer: 'not the fruit of experience, but experience itself, is the end'. It is for this reason that to be asked in the midst of an intense æsthetic impression 'whether one likes it', is like a somnambulist being called by name: it is a recall to one's concrete self, an awakening of practical consciousness which throws the whole æsthetic mechanism out of gear. One might almost venture upon the paradox that the more intense the æsthetic absorption, the less one 'likes', consciously, the experience. The failure to realise this fact, so fully borne out by all genuine artistic experience, is the fundamental error of hedonistic Æsthetics.

The problem of the relation of the beautiful and the agreeable has taken more definite shape in the question of the æsthetic value of the so-called 'lower senses' (comprising sensations of taste and temperature, muscular and tactile, and organic sensations). Sight and hearing have always been the 'æsthetic senses' *par excellence*. Scent has been admitted to the status of an æsthetic sense by some, excluded by others. The ground for the rejection of the lower senses has always been that they mediate only agreeable sensations,

[1] G. Allen, *Physiological Æsthetics*, 1897.
[2] H. R. Marshall, *Pain, Pleasure and Æsthetics*, 1894; *Æsthetic Principles*, 1895.

but are incapable of conveying æsthetic experiences. Though true normally, this rigid distinction is theoretically unfair to the senses, and in practice often false. It is undoubtedly very difficult to reach an æsthetic appreciation through the lower senses, because the materialness of their action, their proximity and bodily connection are great obstacles to their distancing. The aroma of coffee may be a kind of foretaste, taste etherialised, but still a taste. The sweetness of scent of a rose is usually felt more as a bodily caress than as an æsthetic experience. Yet poets have not hesitated to call the scents of flowers their 'souls'. Shelley has transformed the scent to an imperceptible sound.[1] We call such conceptions 'poetical': they mark the transition from the merely agreeable to the beautiful by means of Distance.

M. Guyau, in a well-known passage,[2] has described the same transformation of a taste. Even muscular sensations may present æsthetic possibilities, in the free exercise of bodily movement, the swing of a runner, in the ease and certainty of the trained gymnast; nay, such diffuse organic sensations as the buoyancy of well-being, and the elasticity of bodily energy, can, in privileged moments, be æsthetically enjoyed. That they admit of no material fixation, such as objects of sight and hearing do, and for that reason form no part of Art in the narrower sense; that they exist as æsthetic objects only for the moment and for the single being that enjoys them, is no argument against their æsthetic character. Mere material existence and permanence is no æsthetic criterion.

This is all the more true, as even among the experiences of lasting things, such as are generally accounted to yield æsthetic impressions, the merely agreeable occurs as frequently as the beautiful.

To begin with the relatively simple case of colour-appreciation. Most people imagine that because they are not colour-blind, physically or spiritually, and prefer to live in a coloured world

[1] Cf. 'The Sensitive Plant'.
[2] M. Guyau, *Problèmes de l'Esthétique contemporaine*, Paris, 1897, 4me éd. Livre I, chap. VI.

rather than in an engraving, they possess an æsthetic appreciation
of colour as such. This is the sort of fallacy which hedonistic art-
theories produce, and the lack of an exchange of views on the
subject only fosters. Everybody believes that he enjoys colour—
and for that matter other things—just like anyone else. Yet rather
the contrary is the case. By far the greater number, when asked
why they like a colour, will answer, that they like it, because it
strikes them as warm or cold, stimulating or soothing, heavy or
light. They constitute a definite type of colour-appreciation and
form about sixty per cent of all persons. The remainder assumes,
for the greater part, a different attitude. Colours do not appeal to
them as effects (largely organic) upon themselves. Their appreciation attributes to colours a kind of personality: colours are ener-
getic, lively, serious, pensive, melancholic, affectionate, subtle,
reserved, stealthy, treacherous, brutal, etc. These characters are
not mere imaginings, left to the whim of the individual, romancing whatever he pleases into the colours, nor are they the work
simply of accidental associations. They follow, on the contrary,
definite rules in their applications; they are, in fact, the same
organic effects as those of the former type, but transformed into,
or interpreted as, attributes of the colour, instead of as affections of
one's own self. In short, they are the result of the distancing of the
organic effects: they form an æsthetic appreciation of colour,
instead of a merely agreeable experience like those of the former
kind.[1]

A similar parallelism of the agreeable and the beautiful (in the
widest sense of æsthetic value) occurs also within the sphere of
recognised art-forms. I select for special notice *comedy* and *melodrama* (though the same observation can be made in painting,
architecture and notably in music), firstly as counterparts to
tragedy, discussed earlier, secondly, because both represent admitted art-forms, in spite of their, at least partially, inadequate
claims to the distinction, and lastly because all these types, tragedy,

---

[1] Cf. E. Bullough, 'The Perceptive Problem in the Æsthetic Appreciation of
Single Colours', *British Journal of Psychology*, 1908, II, 406 ff.

comedy and melodrama, are usually grouped together as 'arts of the theatre' no less than as forms of 'literature'.

From the point of view of the present discussion, the case of *comedy* is particularly involved. What we mean by comedy as a class of theatrical entertainment covers several different kinds,[1] which actually merge into each other and present historically a continuity which allows of no sharp lines of demarcation (a difficulty, by the way, which besets all distinctions of literary or artistic *species*, as opposed to artistic *genera*). The second difficulty is that the 'laughable' includes much more than the comic of comedy. It may enter, in all its varieties of the ridiculous, silly, naïve, brilliant, especially as the humorous, into comedy as ingredients, but the comic is not coextensive with the laughable as a whole.

The fact to be noted here is that the different types of comedy, as well as the different kinds of the laughable, presuppose different degrees of Distance. Their tendency is to have none at all. Both to laugh and to weep are direct expressions of a thoroughly practical nature, indicating almost always a concrete personal affection. Indeed, given suitable circumstances and adequate distancing-power, both can be distanced, but only with great difficulty; nor is it possible to decide which of the two offers the greater difficulty. The balance seems almost to incline in favour of tears as the easier of the two, and this would accord with the acknowledged difficulty of producing a really good comedy, or of maintaining a consistent æsthetic attitude in face of a comic situation. Certainly the tendency to *under*-distance is more felt in comedy even than in

---

[1] Comedy embraces *satirical comedy*, i.e. dramatic invectives of all degrees of personal directness, from the attack on actually existing persons (such as is prohibited by the censorship, but has flourished everywhere) to skits upon existing professions, customs, evils, or society; secondly, *farce* rarely unmixed with satire, but occasionally *pure* nonsense and horseplay; thirdly, *comedy proper*, a sublimation of farce into the pure comedy of general human situation, or genuine character-comedy, changing easily into the fourth class, the type of play described on the Continent as *drama* (in the narrower sense), i.e. a play involving serious situations, sometimes with tragic prospects, but having an happy, if often unexpected, ending.

tragedy; most types of the former presenting a *non-distanced*, practical and personal appeal, which precisely implies that their enjoyment is generally hedonic, not æsthetic. In its lower forms comedy consequently is a mere amusement and falls as little under the heading of Art as pamphleteering would be considered as *belles-lettres*, or a burglary as a dramatic performance. It may be spiritualised, polished and refined to the sharpness of a dagger-point or the subtlety of foil-play, but there still clings to it an atmosphere of amusement pure and simple, sometimes of a rude, often of a cruel kind. This, together with the admitted preference of comedy for generalised types rather than for individualised figures, suggests the conclusion that its point of view is the survival of an attitude which the higher forms of Art have outgrown. It is noteworthy that this tendency decreases with every step towards high comedy, character-comedy and drama, with the growing spiritualisation of the comic elements and the first appearance of Distance. Historically the development has been slow and halting. There is no doubt that the seventeenth century considered the *Misanthrope* as amusing. We are nowadays less harsh and less socially intolerant and Alceste appears to us no longer as frankly ridiculous. The supreme achievement of comedy is unquestionably that 'distanced ridicule' which we call *humour*. This self-contradiction of smiling at what we love, displays, in the light vein, that same perfect and subtle balance of the 'antinomy of Distance' which the truly tragic shows in the serious mood. The tragic and the humorous are the genuine æsthetic opposites; the tragic and the comic are contradictory in the matter of Distance, as æsthetic and hedonic objects respectively.

A similar hedonic opposition in the other direction is to be found between tragedy and *melodrama*. Whereas comedy tends to *under*-distance, melodrama suffers from *over*-distancing. For a cultivated audience its overcharged idealism, the crude opposition of vice and virtue, the exaggeration of its underlined moral, its innocence of *nuance*, and its sentimentality with violin-accompaniment are sufficient cause to stamp it as inferior Art. But perhaps its excessive distance is the least Distance obtainable by the public for which it is designed, and may be a great help to an unsophisticated audience in distancing the characters and events. For it is more than probable that we make a mistake in assuming an analogy between a cultivated audience at a serious drama and a melodramatic audience. It is very likely that the lover of melo-drama does not present that subtle balance of mind towards a play, implied in the 'antinomy of Distance'. His attitude is rather either that of a matter-of-fact adult or of a child: i.e. he is either in a frankly personal relation to the events of the play and would like to cudgel the villain who ill-treats the innocent heroine, and rejoices loudly in his final defeat—just as he would in real life—or he is completely lost in the excessive distance imposed by the work and watches naïvely the wonders he sees, as a child listens en-chantedly to a fairy-tale. In neither case is his attitude æsthetic; in the one the object is *under-*, in the other *over-*distanced; in the former he confuses it with the reality he *knows* (or thinks he knows) to exist, in the other with a reality whose existence he does *not know, but accepts*. Neither bears the twofold character of the æsthetic state in which *we know* a thing *not* to exist, but *accept its existence*. From the point of view of moral advantage—in the absence of any æsthetic advantage—the former attitude might seem preferable. But even this may be doubted; for if he believes what he sees in a great spectacular melodrama, every marble-lined hall of the most ordinary London hotel that he passes after the play must appear to him as a veritable Hell, and every man or woman in evening-dress as the devil incarnate. On either sup-position, the moral effect must be deplorable in the extreme, and the melodrama is generally a much more fitting object of the censor's attention than any usually censored play. For in the one case the brutalising effect of the obtrusively visible wickedness cannot possibly be outweighed by any retaliatory poetic justice, which must seem to him singularly lacking in real life; in the other, the effect is purely negative and narcotic; in both his perspective of real life is hopelessly outfocused and distorted.

2. The importance of Distance in artistic creation has already been briefly alluded to in connection with the 'antinomy of Distance'.

Distancing might, indeed, well be considered as the especial and primary function of what is called the 'creative act' in artistic production: distancing is the *formal* aspect of creation in Art. The view that the artist 'copies nature' has already been dismissed. Since the 'imitation-of-nature' theory was officially discarded at the beginning of the nineteenth century, its place in popular fancy has been taken by the conception of the 'self-expression of the artist', supported by the whole force of the Romantic Movement in Europe. Though true as a crude statement of the subjective origin of an artistic conception, though in many ways preferable to its predecessor and valuable as a corollary of such theories as that of the 'organic growth' of a work of Art, it is apt to lead to confusions and to one-sided inferences, to be found even in such deliberate and expert accounts of artistic production as that of Benedetto Croce.[1] For, to start with, the 'self-expression' of an artist is not such as the 'self-expression' of a letter-writer or a public speaker: it is not the *direct* expression of the concrete personality of the artist; it is not even an *indirect* expression of his concrete personality, in the sense in which, for instance, Hamlet's 'self-expression' might be supposed to be the indirect reflection of Shakespeare's ideas. Such a denial, it might be argued, runs counter to the observation that in the works of a literary artist, for example, are to be found echoes and mirrorings of his times and of his personal experiences and convictions. But it is to be noted that to find these *is* in fact impossible, unless you previously know what reflections to look for. Even in the relatively most direct transference from personal experiences to their expression, viz. in lyrical poetry, such a connection cannot be established backwards, though it is easy enough to prove it forwards: i.e. given the knowledge of the experiences, there is no difficulty in tracing their

[1] Benedetto Croce, *Æsthetic*, translated by Douglas Ainslie, Macmillan, 1909.

echoes, but it is impossible to infer biographical data of any detail or concrete value from an author's works alone. Otherwise Shakespeare's *Sonnets* would not have proved as refractory to biographical research as they have done, and endless blunders in literary history would never have been committed. What proves so impossible in literature, which after all offers an exceptionally adequate medium to 'self-expression', is *a fortiori* out of question in other arts, in which there is not even an equivalence between the personal experiences and the material in which they are supposed to be formulated. The fundamental two-fold error of the 'self-expression' theory is to speak of 'expression' in the sense of 'intentional communication', and to identify straightway the artìst and the man. An intentional communication is as far almost from the mind of the true artist as it would be from that of the ordinary respectable citizen to walk about naked in the streets, and the idea has repeatedly been indignantly repudiated by artists. The second confusion is as misleading in its theoretical consequences, as it is mischievous and often exceedingly painful to the 'man' as well as to the 'artist'. The numberless instances in history of the astonishing difference, often the marked contrast between the *man* and his *work*, is one of the most disconcerting riddles of Art, and should serve as a manifest warning against the popular illusion of finding the 'artist's mind' in his productions.[1]

Apart from the complication of technical necessities, of conventional art-forms, of the requirements of unification and composition, all impeding the direct transference of an actual mental content into its artistic formulation, there is the interpolation of Distance which stands between the artist's conception and the man's. For the 'artist' himself is already distanced from the concrete, historical personality, who ate and drank and slept and did the ordinary business of life. No doubt here also are *degrees* of Distance, and the 'antinomy' applies to this case too. Some figures in literature and other arts are unquestionably self-portraits; but

---

[1] Some well-known examples of this difference are, for instance: Mozart, Beethoven, Watteau, Murillo, Molière, Schiller, Verlaine, Zola.

even self-portraits are not, and cannot be, the direct and faithful cast taken from the living soul. In short, so far from being 'self-expression', *artistic production is the indirect formulation of a distanced mental content.*

I give a short illustration of this fact. A well-known dramatist described to me the process of production as taking place in his case in some such way as follows:

The starting-point of his production is what he described as an 'emotional idea', i.e. some more or less general conception carrying with it a strong emotional tone. This idea may be suggested by an actual experience; anyhow the idea itself *is* an actual experience, i.e. it occurs within the range of his normal, practical being. Gradually it condenses itself into a situation made up of the interplay of certain characters, which may be of partly objective, partly imaginative descent. Then ensues what he describes as a 'life and death struggle' between the idea and the characters for existence: if the idea gains the upper hand, the conception of the whole is doomed. In the successful issue, on the contrary, the idea is, to use his phrase, 'sucked up' by the characters as a sponge sucks up water, until no trace of the idea is left outside the characters. It is a process, which, he assured me, he is quite powerless to direct or even to influence. It is further of interest to notice that during this period the idea undergoes sometimes profound, often wholesale changes. Once the stage of complete fusion of the idea with the characters is reached, the conscious elaboration of the play can proceed. What follows after this, is of no further interest in this connection.

This account tallies closely with the procedure which numerous dramatists are known to have followed. It forms a definite type. There are other types, equally well supported by evidence, which proceed along much less definite lines of a semi-logical development, but rather show sudden flash-like illuminations and much more subconscious growth.

The point to notice is the 'life and death struggle' between the idea and the characters. As I first remarked, the idea is the *'man's'*, it is the reflection of the dramatist's concrete and practical self. Yet this is precisely the part which must 'die'. The paradox of just the germ-part of the whole being doomed, particularly impressed my informant as a kind of life-tragedy. The 'characters' on the other hand belong to the imaginary world, to the 'artist's'. Though they may be partially suggested by actuality, their full-grown development is divorced from it. This process of the 'idea' being 'sucked up' by the characters and being destroyed by it, is a phase of artistic production technically known as the 'objectivation' of the conception. In it the 'man' dies and the 'artist' comes to life, and with him the work of Art. It is a change of death and birth in which there is no overlapping of the lives of parent and child. The result is the distanced finished production. As elsewhere, the distancing means the separation of personal affections, whether idea or complex experience, from the concrete personality of the experiencer, its filtering by the extrusion of its personal aspects, the throwing out of gear of its personal potency and significance.

The same transformation through distance is to be noticed in *acting*. Here, even more than in the other arts, a lingering bias in favour of the 'imitation of nature' theory has stood in the way of correct interpretation of the facts. Yet acting supplies in this and other respects exceptionally valuable information, owing to its medium of expression and the overlapping—at least in part—of the process of producing with the finished production, which elsewhere are separated in point of time. It illustrates, as no other art can, the cleavage between the concrete, normal person and the distanced personality. [The acting here referred to is, of course, not that style which consists in 'walking on'. What is meant here is 'creative' acting, which in its turn must be distinguished from 'reproductive' acting—two different types traceable through the greater part of theatrical history, which in their highest development are often outwardly indistinguishable, but nevertheless retain traces of differences, characteristic of their procedures and psychical mechanism.] This cleavage between the two streams or layers of consciousness is so obvious that it has led to increasing speculation from the time when acting first attracted intelligent interest, since the middle of the eighteenth century. From the time of Diderot's *Paradoxe sur le Comédien* (itself only the last of a series of French studies) down to Mr. William Archer's *Masks or Faces* (1888) and the controversy between Coquelin and Salvini (in the nineties), theory has been at pains to grapple with this phenomenon. Explanations have differed widely, going from the one extreme of an identification of the acting and the normal personality to the other of a separation so wide as to be theoretically inconceivable and contradicted by experience. It is necessary to offer some conception which will account for the differences as well as for the indirect connection between the two forms of being, and which is applicable not merely to acting, but to other kinds of art as well. Distance, it is here contended, meets the requirement even in its subtlest shades. To show this in detail lies outside the scope of this essay, and forms rather the task of a special treatment of the psychology of acting.

[3. In the interest of those who may be familiar with the developments of æsthetic theories of late years, I should like to add that Distance has a special bearing upon many points raised by them. It is essential to the occurrence and working of 'empathy' (*Einfühlung*), and I mentioned earlier its connection with Witasek's theory of *Scheingefühle* which forms part of his view on 'empathy'. The distinction between sympathy and 'empathy' as formulated by Lipps[1] is a matter of the relative degree of Distance. Volkelt's[2] suggestion of regarding the ordinary apprehension of expression (say of a person's face) as the first rudimentary stage of *Einfühlung*, leading subsequently to the lowering of our consciousness of reality ('*Herabsetzung des Wirklichkeitsgefühls*'), can similarly be formulated in terms of Distance. K. Lange's[3] account of æsthetic experience in the form of 'illusion as conscious self-deception'

[1] Th. Lipps, *Æsthetik*, Hamburg and Leipzig, 1903, I; '*Æsthetische Einfühlung*', *Ztsch. für Psychol. u. Physiol. der Sinnesorg.*, XXII, 415 ff.

[2] J. Volkelt, *System der Æsthetik*, 1905, I, 217 ff. and 488 ff.

[3] K. Lange, *Das Wesen der Kunst*, 1901, 2 vols.

appears to me a wrong formulation of the facts expressed by Distance. Lange's 'illusion' theory seems to me, among other things,[1] to be based upon a false opposition between Art and reality (nature) as the subject-matter of the former, whereas Distance does not imply any comparison between them in the act of experiencing and removes altogether the centre of gravity of the formula from the opposition.]

4. In this way Distance represents in æsthetic appreciation as well as in artistic production a quality inherent in the impersonal, yet *so* intensely personal, relation which the human being entertains with Art, either as mere beholder or as producing artist.

It is Distance which makes the æsthetic object 'an end in itself'. It is that which raises Art beyond the narrow sphere of individual interest and imparts to it that 'postulating' character which the idealistic philosophy of the nineteenth century regarded as a metaphysical necessity. It renders questions of origin, of influences, or of purposes almost as meaningless as those of marketable value, of pleasure, even of moral importance, since it lifts the work of Art out of the realm of practical systems and ends.

In particular, it is Distance which supplies one of the special criteria of æsthetic values as distinct from practical (utilitarian), scientific, or social (ethical) values. All these are concrete values, either *directly* personal as utilitarian, or *indirectly* remotely personal, as moral values. To speak, therefore, of the 'pleasure value' of Art, and to introduce hedonism into æsthetic speculation, is even more irrelevant than to speak of moral hedonism in Ethics. Æsthetic hedonism is a compromise. It is the attempt to reconcile for public use utilitarian ends with æsthetic values. Hedonism, as a practical, personal appeal, has no place in the distanced appeal of Art. Moral hedonism is even more to the point than æsthetic hedonism, since ethical values, *qua* social values, lie on the line of prolongation of utilitarian ends, sublimating indeed the *directly* personal object into the realm of socially or universally valuable ends, often demanding

[1] J. Segal, 'Die bewusste Selbsttäuschung als Kern des æsthetischen Geniessens', *Arch. f. d. ges. Psychol.*, VI, 254 ff.

the sacrifice of individual happiness, but losing neither its *practical* nor even its *remotely personal* character.

In so far, Distance becomes one of the distinguishing features of the 'æsthetic consciousness', of that special mentality or outlook upon experience and life, which, as I said at the outset, leads in its most pregnant and most fully developed form, both appreciatively and productively, to Art.

# Mind and Medium in Art

[This was the fourth of five contributions to a Symposium
on this theme presented at the Congress of Philosophy in
Oxford, 24–27 September 1920, and published in the
*British Journal of Psychology*, vol. XI, 1. The first contributor,
Mr. Charles Marriott, taking the line that art is primarily
the technical manipulation of a medium, and æsthetic
appreciation a sense of practical problems efficiently solved,
ends inevitably by asserting that the difference between a
house-painter and Michelangelo is one of degree not of
kind. Mr. A. B. Walkley arrives at the same conclusion,
that all men are artists in some degree, but by starting from
precisely the opposite end: with the Crocean thesis that art
is essentially mind, the medium having no æsthetic significance but serving only the practical function of communication. Mr. H. J. Watt, protesting against attempts to build an
æsthetic theory without taking every art into consideration,
concentrates on music. He objects equally to the nebulous-
ness of the Crocean formula, that art is an 'expression of
intuition', and to biologistic attempts to turn it into a
utilitarian practice just because it originated in the useful
crafts. The fifth contribution was a summing-up by
Professor C. W. Valentine. Ed.]

I agree with Mr. Walkley's criticism of Mr. Marriott's proposal to base an æsthetic theory upon Medium and its technical manipulation. The attempt has been made more than once—the example of Semper has been mentioned by Mr. Watt—and has always broken down in the face of objections such as are urged by Mr. Walkley —in the last resort because Art is a manifestation of mind and cannot be satisfactorily accounted for by the nature and treatment of the material it employs.

The second part of Mr. Walkley's paper rests upon the theory of Benedetto Croce. I am in doubt how far I agree or disagree with him. Croce's æsthetic theory does not stand by itself, as is far too commonly supposed. It is part of a general philosophical, and in addition monistic, system and is exposed to all the difficulties created by such a dependence. I feel doubt about the fourfold division of the activities of the spirit; about the precise limits of the theoretical and practical activities; about the ultimate implications of his general point of view; as regards the æsthetic sphere in particular, about the nature of the 'intuition' and the essential 'lyricism' of Art, and their consequences. Indeed, I am inclined to agree with the objections recently urged by G. A. Borgese in the Preface to the new edition of his *Storia della critica romantica in Italia*.[1] I readily admit that Croce's conception of intuition as the

---

[1] Treves, Milano, 1920, p. xix f. [Bullough gave his quotation in Italian; I have replaced it by this rendering. Ed.] 'The development of the so-called Romantic criticism had found its culmination in De Sanctis. Two ways now remained open: either to actuate further and more resolutely the restoration of classical feeling in art which, paradoxically enough, was called Romanticism in Italy or, through this pseudo-Romanticism, to arrive at a real Romanticism.

'Croce committed himself, without marked indecision, to this second road and became more and more confirmed in his view of art as instinct, as "Genie", as irreducible individualism, as "hohe Intuition" preceding both logic and will, as pure lyricism, as an interjection and a cry. His critical method became more and more the exact expression of three principles: (1) to deny any continuity of development in art history, which he broke down into monads without, however, allowing windows for the single poetic individualities; (2) to seek in every poet his genuine and fundamental work, generally that belonging to his first and spontaneous youth, and to reject as logical and wishful superimpositions his pretended development in

kernel of the artistic attitude, his antagonism to the current treatment of the history of Art and to the sterile discussions of the
differences and relative position of the arts, and his insistence on
the unity and uniqueness of Art, etc., have rendered immense
services to æsthetic studies; yet I cannot but feel a certain sympathy
with the complaint of Professor Bosanquet (with whose æsthetic
views I otherwise disagree) that Croce's theory yields little en-
lightenment on the particular subject now under discussion.
Croce's theory is a philosophical, not a psychological, statement,
and there is much that seems psychologically obscure in it. More-
over, the subject of the present debate is in itself, as a matter of
psychological fact, so obscure that its elucidation would appear to
me as little furthered by a philosophical treatment which deals
with it from an ideal point of view, as by Mr. Marriott's hypo-
thetical illustrations which substitute assumptions for experience.

I. What do we actually know about the relation of Mind and
Medium in Art?

By *Medium* I assume we mean the material or physical datum
which the artist handles: paint and canvas; chalk and paper;
marble or bronze; brick or stone or concrete; the tones of an
instrument or the human voice; the human body, its gestures and
attitudes, whether in actual space as in dancing or acting, or in
imaginary space as in the cinematograph film.

By *Technique* I mean the manipulation of these media.

The *Mind* refers, I take it, to the mind of the artist as well as of
the spectator or listener (recipient), but chiefly to the former.

As regards the term *Art*, I must beg leave to make one or two
more extensive observations. In the first place we would, I believe,
all agree that Art represents but a segment of the whole range of
æsthetic activity. The æsthetic attitude embraces the appreciation

maturity; (3) to read every poet and every work as an anthology, in which a
few lyric fragments have been artificially sewn together in the extra-æsthetic
delusion of achieving a unity. His recent essays in particular, especially the one
on Goethe, show his determination to submit almost every play, almost every
poem to that disrupting analysis which Romantic philology attempted on the
Homeric poems.'

of natural objects as well as of artefacts; it covers certain border-
lands of Art such as ceremonial and ritual which have admittedly
artistic affinities; it permeates ordinary human intercourse in what
we vaguely call 'manners'. As a matter of personal conviction, I
hold that there is nothing in the whole range of personal experience from sheer sense-experience to the most abstract thought
which may not be the object of æsthetic contemplation. To speak
of medium in this case becomes exceedingly difficult, because the
medium is, I presume, one's very self—as, in fact, it is in certain
types of acting: *la plastique de l'âme*. Of this vast realm of sometimes most tenuous and elusive experience, the title restricts us to
the most condensed—if I may use a contradiction in terms—the
most material, but also the most deliberate and most intentional
form of the æsthetic state.

II. Further, I believe it to be important to point out the distinction between *Art in its static* and *Art in its dynamic aspect*. The distinction is important because, though it is constantly overlooked,
it affects the relation between mind and medium in several
particulars, and incidentally also the conception of a history of
Art, the interplay of social and individual factors and the continuity of artistic and æsthetic tradition.

By Art in its static aspect I mean what I cannot do better than
describe as 'the objective world of Art', i.e. the accumulations of
art-treasures in our museums and collections, the art-*objects* as
material things, independently of all considerations of their subjective origins, the intentions and ideals of their creators; independently also of our æsthetic attitude to them, regarded merely
as objects, as remains of antiquity or illustrations of the past.

Art in its dynamic aspect is Art regarded from the point of view
of the creative artist or actively appreciating recipient: as an
æsthetic object. There is of course a constant interchange between
these two conceptions of Art. An art-object which today is
dynamic for me, may tomorrow have become static. A picture
may one day belong in my eyes to the objective world of Art and
the next day may assume a dynamic aspect. To say that as a static

object it had no æsthetic existence for me, is of course true—that is precisely the distinction—yet I knew all along that it was an art-object and was regarded as such by others for whom it had become dynamic. And its claim to become dynamic for me also was there with it and exercised a certain moulding influence upon my æsthetic attitude. This silent, collective and largely anonymous pressure of the 'objective world of Art' is probably the most potent agency in the art-education of the individual. It represents in its cumulative force, created by the forgotten but combined verdict of past generations—to whom it also owes its preservation—a tremendous standardising power upon the schooling of appreciation and produces adaptations, expectancies, apperceptions and emotional reactions which in their varying degree of rigidity and durability result in more or less fixed habits of taste. This applies to generations as well as individuals. The 'objective world of Art' and dynamic Art are naturally never co-extensive. For the majority of persons the vast number of art-objects never become dynamic; but the appeal to become so remains and is satisfied in proportion to the powers of imagination, the emotional elasticity and the extension of the organised interests of the individual appreciator.

The same standardising pressure is exercised upon the artist. The beginnings of every artist are necessarily imitative. What should he imitate but what was there before him? This necessity is reinforced by the capacity of absorption and of admiration which distinguishes the artist as a psychological type. It is further forced upon him by the perpetual technical struggle in which every actively creative artist lives. Defeat in this struggle means incapacity or mannerism. Indeed, it is precisely on the technical side that static Art exercises its strongest influence upon the artist, for it represents the continuity of technical development—distinct from, though not unrelated to, the æsthetic discontinuity of Art history—and technique is the one thing in Art that can be taught —up to a certain point. Incidentally static Art acts as a kind of background for the ricochet of general public sentiment and its attitude towards Art upon the artist, and as a reaction both to this sentiment and to the technical teaching beyond the point where in the artist's development technique ceases to be impersonal, common knowledge and becomes an intimately personal process interwoven with his artistic imagination, static Art becomes the spring-board of reaction, revolt and revolution. For all great artists have been revolutionaries, both in their technique and in their creative work as a whole.

In this manner, the objective world of Art, by reason of its persistence, has in a sense a survival value, and as the expression of certain forms of historical continuity, represents for the artist and the appreciator a kind of collective and socially-conditioned standard and—up to the above-mentioned point—a similarly socially-conditioned, impersonal technical tradition.

As constituent elements of the objective world of Art we encounter the various 'arts' and crafts, as historically they have arisen, developed and differentiated themselves in their materials, techniques, styles and ideals, and have created different professional habits of thoughts and tastes and distinct expectations and anticipated standards in their respective devotees. Art as the formulation of a unique and distinct psychological attitude is unquestionably ONE, and these different art-forms, as I should prefer to call them, appear largely as the outcome of accidents of history, climate, habitat, economic conditions, inventions, cultures, and in the last resort, of our physiological constitution. But they are for all that æsthetically not irrelevant, however little result the past discussions on their æsthetic differences and relations have yielded. The error lay in regarding them as fixed, predetermined and logically deducible species, each with its own 'laws' and 'principles'. The art-forms which we know and distinguish conventionally, are not, of course, the only 'arts'. In other countries, at other times, activities which we do not regard as a form of art were reckoned among the arts and vice versa. It is the subjective attitude which recognises certain activities as art-forms, and the equally subjective repercussion exercised by them, once (and while) they are so recognised, which make the 'arts' æsthetically relevant. Even at the present time we are witnessing in the development of the cinema-film, however much prostituted for the moment, the rise of an entirely new 'art', and there is no limit but that of our physiological constitution to æsthetic imagination and its inter-action with non-æsthetic inventions for the production of material art-forms. Nor is there ultimately any limit at all to the range of subject-matter of the æsthetic psychosis[1] itself. The 'arts' are merely the forms of 'exteriorisation' which in the course of history have been relatively distinct and continuous strands in the art-tradition of mankind.

The influence of the media in producing changes in the tech-nical procedures and thereby in the historical styles of the art-forms is so well known as to require but mere mention. The effect of small units of building materials upon the development of architectural forms and eventually upon the growth of the Gothic style; of Roman cement upon Roman vault construction; of rein-forced concrete upon the structural problems and architectural forms of the present day are notorious instances in Architecture. Equally well known is the influence of tempera upon certain characteristics of Italian Renaissance painting and the changes introduced into the art by the use of oil-pigments. Comparable to the ease and freedom of oil-painting have been the effects of the development of the piano on music, and the similarities of the consequences, both good and bad, have frequently been noticed. The differences between the use of marble and bronze in Sculpture, whether in the round or in relief, are to be found in every text-book on ancient Sculpture. The peculiarities of French verse in contrast to English, German, Italian and Russian are due for the largest part to the absence of a marked stress accent in the French language, and the use of intricate classical metres in English poetry is practically impossible because the language is so largely mono-syllabic. Changes in the shape of the stage and in its relation to the

[1 Cf. p. 150, fn. 1. Ed.]

audience, in decoration, *mise en scène* and personnel reacted on the nature of 'theatrical illusion', types of play and the whole style of acting. The transition from the Commedia dell' arte to the regular drama had its repercussion on the psychology of the actor.

It would be easy to multiply *ad infinitum* such influences of media upon the art-forms. The point I wish to make here is that in changing the forms and traditional styles of the arts the effects of the different media are crystallised and incorporated by means of their techniques in the objective arts and, as stated before in more general terms, come inevitably to form the basis for the technical rudiments of the budding artist and set up new standards of technical handling in the mind of the recipient. One cannot but be impressed—whether favourably or not—with the profound imprint, for instance, of the 'classical orders' upon the mind of the architectural student, ever since Vitruvius has become the bible of the 'classical' architect. The extent and depth to which the student's vision is moulded by the shape, dimensions and proportions and formal functions of these orders is enormous with the cumulative force of century-old training on these lines. This is perhaps an extreme instance of the pressure of historical style, but similar results, if in smaller degree, will be found in other art-forms.

Mr. Watt points out that the musical instrument and its technique is an important condition of 'style' in music. Indeed, 'style' has often been defined as the consistent treatment of a particular medium. This is true, if by style is meant what I have here called 'historical style'. But style in the purely artistic sense is not the consistent treatment of an impersonal, physical medium any more than technique is Art, but a consistency in the artist's personal vision, 'consistency of distance' as I have called it elsewhere.[1] The manipulation of the material medium enters into this vision, no doubt; but it is not, either directly or by itself, the basis of 'style'.

III. What is the process by which the medium enters into this vision of the artist? This question leads to the consideration of

[1] *British Journal of Psychology*, **v.**

Art in its dynamic aspect, i.e. to artistic creation and æsthetic appreciation.

What is the dynamic relation of the artist to his medium?

By way of apology for much that I have said above, I venture to submit that nearly all æsthetic theory of the past and of the present seems to me exposed to the serious criticism that it deals with the artist, so to say, *in vacuo*, psychologically and philosophically, without any reference whatever to the social unit, social relations and interactions in which he finds himself. This treatment reached its height with the Romantic Movement in Europe, and, as if to redress the balance against this romantic survival in Æsthetics, the type of theory called 'sociological Æsthetics' came into being, with its equally one-sided insistence upon Art as a social manifestation, as an 'expression of society'. This view, usually going back to Taine in some form or other, was supported by the development of scientific thought in the nineteenth century and reinforced by the progress of economic and anthropological studies. The truth seems to lie, as usual, somewhere midway. The artist is not a solitary being, living metaphorically upon a desert island, but is born into a community whose influences he undergoes in common with his fellows. In a sense he does so even more than the others, for a great susceptibility to ideas and the ambient atmosphere and a great power of absorbing them, exceptional both in range and rapidity, are part of his artistic psychological equipment. It is this impressionability which makes him so much more often than his duller brethren the unhappy victim of the herd and, by a natural reaction, into a really solitary person. Yet while *humanly* his contacts with his environment are at least equal to those of his fellows and are usually much more numerous and much less superficial, he is, *qua artist*, undoubtedly infinitely less subject to social pressure than any other member of society, stands infinitely less in need of social co-operation for the exercise of his calling and is almost independent[1] of society in his artistic creation,

---

[1] Apart, of course, from economic considerations.

development and ideals. As artist, he is a kind of imaginative solipsist. The relation of the artist to the Group appears to me consequently as very peculiar and very complex. It has never to my knowledge been satisfactorily dealt with either psychologically or sociologically. Yet it is of fundamental importance to Æsthetics both from the point of view of the artist's psychology and from that of Genetic Æsthetics which has to take count of the historical fluctuations of this relation for an understanding of the history of Art and the development of the æsthetic consciousness formulated in it. Regarding the special problem now before us, I must confine myself to saying that I believe the so-called 'art-conventions' of different ages, which play so important a part in the treatment of media, to be a direct product of this relation.

(a) In its mere material aspect the medium plays a part in this relation, besides the technical tradition which represents one of the chief social influences upon the mind of the artist. The sheer materialness of a medium such, for example, as stone, its durability and conspicuousness, place upon the architect an artistic responsibility towards his contemporaries and posterity which is not borne by other artists in the same way or to the same extent. Building St. Peter's or Westminster Cathedral, building for eternity so to speak, is psychologically a very different proposition to making an etching, composing a song or writing a poem. The permanence or evanescence of a medium invests a work with an atmosphere which reacts upon the psychology both of its creation and its appreciation, and while its *social* importance seems to increase in proportion to the crudeness of the material and the physical labour of its handling, the *individual* preciousness appears to rise to the evanescent tenderness of the human voice or the poignancy of a dramatic scene.—Again the power of experimenting, for instance, evidently decreases with the durability of the material with all the consequences for the psychology of the artist and the technique of the art-form, as in the well-known case of fresco-painting or lithography.—Even the personal relation of the artist to his work is bound to be involved. The poet may destroy his poem, the musician his song, the painter his canvas; they may be forgotten by the public; but building or statue remain to be seen, if not by the artist, yet by the public and become the point at which public feeling impinges upon the self-regarding sentiments of the artist. In a multitude of ways Architecture Sculpture, Painting, Music, Poetry, Acting and Dancing appear as a series of art-forms in which the individual factor assumes ascendingly greater sway over the social determinations, in the freedom from technical tradition, in artistic responsibility, in public resonance; and the medium as sheer physical material seems to play a not inconsiderable part in the complex situation thus created.

(b) I venture to touch in passing upon a point which affects the relation of mind to medium in its more external aspect, viz. the question whether the artist is distinguished by a special sensory sensitiveness towards the medium, superior to that of normal persons. Do painters possess a greater acuity of vision, sculptors a finer sense of touch, etc.? It would appear doubtful, if we allow for the specialised refinement of discrimination due to interest and practice.[1] The problem is obviously difficult to test, but without actual experiment we shall not be much wiser. It would certainly be well worth while to attempt special research on this point as well as on the superiority which training and practice unquestionably confer upon the artist.

(c) On the psychical attitude of the artist to his medium, I had occasion in the course of some experiments on the æsthetic appreciation of colours[2] to make the interesting observation that painters and others professionally interested in colour assumed two entirely different relations to it, according as to whether they viewed it, so to speak, æsthetically or pictorially. As artists they displayed the same attitude which they would assume towards a work of Art; as painters they treated it with a kind of objective detachment

---

[1] Heine und Lenz, *Über Farbensehen, besonders der Kunstmaler*, Jena, 1907.
[2] 'The "Perceptive Problem" in the Æsthetic Appreciation of Simple Colour-Combinations.' *British Journal of Psychology*, III, 444 note.

as a mere, almost indifferent, instrument. The same dualism of attitude will, I think, be found in all arts. The architect or sculptor will feel a thrill of purely æsthetic enjoyment at the beauty of a finely grained stone and will lovingly caress the surface of a beautiful marble; the literary artist will gloat over the sonorousness and rhythm of a word; but each will, when the occasion arises, treat the same object of his delight as part of a completed whole with apparent indifference and will ruthlessly discard it from an unwanted place. And yet something of the intrinsic æsthetic value of the medium will persist as an almost imperceptible diapason in the full harmony of the work. The indifference of his professional attitude is not the indifference of the heedless layman, but the higher detachment which removes the medium from the grossly practical function of a 'materialisation' of his vision into an integral part of it.

(d) The connecting link between the medium and the vision of the artist is *Technique*. The relation described by that term is the adaptation of the medium to the vision, and, vice versa, the adjustment of the vision to the possibilities and exigencies of the medium.

A. (1) Under the first section of this definition we find that Technique consists in the first place in a *knowledge of the medium and of its behaviour*. What is the limit of stress of an arch constructed of a particular material? To what extent will a marble or bronze permit the free detachment of a limb from the body of a statue? What is the range of the human voice? How far will a particular pigment darken in course of time? At the present moment reinforced concrete construction has introduced problems of its own under this heading which are far from solved. Much the greatest part of 'art-education' is concerned with the transmission of the wholly impersonal knowledge of this kind.

(2) As a special part of this knowledge appears the familiarity and practice with the instruments and tools for dealing with the material—a special part, because the invention of new tools has notoriously played so important a role in the history of Art. It was

for that reason that the mythical Daedalids were equally famous as mechanical inventors and as the first artists who 'made men to walk', and we need but scan the technical sections of Vasari to realise the profound preoccupation of the Renaissance artists over the mechanical problems presented by the media of their day. A History of Art dealing pre-eminently with the modifications introduced by the invention of new tools and processes—in its repercussion upon the mind of the artists—would fill a gaping lacuna in our present knowledge and understanding of the development of Art, especially in its earlier phases.

(3) Knowledge of the nature and behaviour of the medium and of the functions of the tools for its manipulation will remain a mere impersonal 'knowledge by description' unless and until it is converted into active and personal familiarity by practice. The object of all practice is the acquisition of *manual dexterity*, if I may use 'manual' generically to indicate the muscular and motor-training whether actually of the hand, or of the control of voice, gesture, facial expression or even the remoter accuracy and spontaneity of auditive imagery, whether musical or linguistic. The ideal is 'la man che ubbedisce all' intelletto' of Michelangelo, the perfect and minutely correct adjustment of muscular action to impulses of the will and even its unconscious control. This manual dexterity is the first prerequisite of any artist and is, in distinction to mere knowledge, transmissible only in the smallest part. The degree of perfection in the control of muscular movements that can be achieved is well known from the numberless stories told of most of the great artists of the past. Manual dexterity of this kind is one of the main differences distinguishing the artist from the merely appreciative layman. Though apparently nothing more (though often wellnigh incredible at that) than quasi-mechanical tricks—and a good deal of it is constantly mistaken for Art—it is the foundation, practically and psychologically, upon which great Art must necessarily build; practically, because it is the condition of the power over the material; psychologically, because it constitutes a personal knowledge of the limits and the possibilities of

the medium which through the formation of technical habits comes to modify the artist's vision itself.

(4) Manual dexterity would be inconceivable without what I should like to call 'technical memory'. What I mean by technical memory is the accurate persistence in memory of the—presumably muscular—adjustments which enable for instance the actor to reproduce, perhaps after years, the same voice-inflection in a particular sentence, or enabled Giotto on a famous occasion to draw a perfect circle free-hand. I have heard it said that in the last works of Beethoven the use of the human voice occasionally shows signs of a slight hesitation, due to the years of deafness with which he was afflicted. This would be an instance of the weakening of what I mean by technical memory. The existence of a technical memory, apart from its obvious necessity for the development of manual dexterity, is an essential condition to the exercise of technical imagination (see below).

B. If we consider the relation described by 'Technique' from the other, the mind-end, so to speak, we find, I believe, that it consists principally of the *knowledge of the effects* which can be achieved by the handling of a particular medium, a knowledge acquired, perfected and refined, of course, by the combined familiarity with the medium and the practice in its manipulation.

We encounter at this point a problem which I can mention only in passing. It appears in its acutest form in such art-forms as Architecture and Sculpture, though it seems to arise equally in the other arts. What is the difference between Building and Architecture or between a cast taken from a living body and a piece of Sculpture? The matter has been dealt with in the well-known book of A. Hildebrand, *Das Problem der Form in der bildenden Kunst.*[1] The point here is that in Architecture, for instance, the structure, the material form with all its technical problems, is, as it were, merely the substratum of the *spatial* forms which Archi-

---

[1] Jena, 1905 (5th ed.). There exists an American translation of the book, but the translation introduces an eye-movement theory foreign to the intentions of the original.

tecture endeavours to produce and render effective. These two forms, the structural and the spatial forms, are by no means identical. The structural form may at times coincide with the spatial form, but very often the spatial form is quite different from, though produced by, the structural form. A column, structurally, carries a load and is the transmission of a *downward* stress; spatially, it is a *rising* form. Well-known instances are the usual geometrical-optical illusions, and, while Building is the science of structure, Architecture is the art of three-dimensional optical illusions. The architect aims deliberately at the production of (or correction of undesirable) optical spatial illusions by means of the structural forms. Hence the fundamental importance of knowing what effects will or will not be produced by particular material forms in particular positions, perspectives, foreshortenings, lights, colours, etc. The same applies, *mutatis mutandis*, to Sculpture and all the other arts.

This is the point at which the vision of the artist is profoundly affected by the medium, for unless *the vision is conceived in terms of the medium*, it would be almost an abuse of language to call it vision at all. This influence penetrates the vision in its minutest details, in proportion to the perfection of the adaptation between the mind and the medium, i.e. of the technique of the artist. It is a crude but well-known illustration that a statue cannot be conceived in marble and executed in bronze. As has been pointed out by Max Klinger,[1] it makes all the difference whether a picture is designed as an etching or as a mezzotint, i.e. whether you work from light to dark or from dark to light. The sculptural vision depends on whether it is to be carried out by modelling or by chiselling—'per via di porre' or 'per forza di levare', as Michelangelo called it. You cannot write a play in prose and later turn it into verse without disturbing the whole relief of it, the interdependence of its parts, the colour of its sentiment and in the last resort the fundamental conception from which it sprang.

[1] Max Klinger, *Malerei und Zeichnung*, Leipzig, 1907 (5th ed.), p. 34 ff.

A failure to achieve this adaptation in the first instance is responsible for the constant corrections and alterations of works in the course of their technical execution, a source of the 'développement par transformation' and 'développement par déviation' of Paulhan.[1] Similarly the reproduction of works in media other than that for which they were designed is bound to be unsatisfactory and can at best have a merely illustrative value.

Lastly the sketches, notes, fragments and uncompleted works of great artists is the most valuable material at our disposal for the study of this interpenetration of medium and mind and are our best evidence for the role played by the medium in the formation of the artist's vision.

Having secured the fact of this interpenetration, we have to raise the question of its mechanism. By far the most illuminating conception here is that of the 'images d'interprétation ou de traduction', suggested by L. Arréat.[2] He writes: 'Un peintre figuriste, qui ne *sait* pas l'animal, a des chevaux à placer dans une composition. Il s'applique alors à l'étude du cheval; il prend des croquis, et se met dans la tête des "images". Un cavalier expert pourra ensuite critiquer son tableau en connaisseur. Il garde donc en mémoire, lui aussi, des images précises, auxquelles il a comparé celles du peintre. Il ne serait pas capable cependant de dessiner un cheval ni de le peindre. A quoi tient précisément cette différence? Il ne suffit pas de dire que c'est faute d'exercice, car la faculté même d'apprendre marque un véritable privilège. C'est d'abord faute d'*images d'interprétation* ou *de traduction*: j'entends par là des schémas visuo-moteurs laissés par l'étude dans le cerveau du peintre, et grâce auxquels sa représentation mentale peut prendre figure aussitôt sur le papier ou la toile—des symboles actifs, en quelque sorte, qui sont comme les idées générales "pittoresques".'

The interest and value of this conception appear to me to lie in the following points:

(1) It seems to me to provide a simple and lucid explanation of

[1] F. Paulhan, *Psychologie de l'invention*, Alcan., 1901.
[2] L. Arréat, *Mémoire et Imagination*, Alcan., 1904, pp. 28–9.

the process whereby practice and study succeed in developing, in the artist as distinct from the layman, both the wealth of memory-images and the facility for executing them.

(2) It gives a rational account of the fusion of the vision and technique and of the effect of technique upon—in the case of the painter—the visual imagery. For these schematic images, or as it were paradigms, forming the stock of the artist's imagery, have been developed in the course of practice and study by the accumulation of images *framed in terms of his medium*.

(3) It emphasises one of the main functions of art-education, viz. the formation and refinement of such 'images de traduction.'[1]

(4) It offers an interesting explanation of what the French call 'la ligne de l'artiste', the 'manner', the almost impalpable peculiarities which distinguish the work of one artist from that of another. They would seem to be reducible to differences in their 'images de traduction',[2] their individual 'pictorial general ideas' under which each subsumes his isolated experiences and impressions. As M. Arréat remarks, a failure to develop, multiply and enrich his 'images de traduction' by constant exercise of observation (and especially imagination) leads to a sterile repetition of these images without individual elaboration: the 'manner' turns to 'mannerism'.

(5) The 'images de traduction' of the painter find their obvious analogies in the other arts, and the same psychological mechanism applies equally to them. Certain attitudes, certain turns of phrase, the use of epithets, the technique of character-portraiture, peculiar musical cadences and harmonies, peculiarities of gesture and voice-inflection for the interpretation of particular emotional states, certain dramatic types—especially the old types of the Commedia dell' Arte—are instances of such 'images de traduction' in Sculpture, Poetry, Music and Drama.

[1] Lecoq de Boisbaudran, *Training of Memory in Art*, Macmillan, 1911.

[2] Ugo Ojetti, the distinguished critic, suggests that the colour-schemes also form part of these 'lignes de l'artiste' (see *Corriere della Sera*, on the occasion of the 400th anniversary of Raffael's death).

So far the relation of mind and medium in regard to the artist up to that point at which he begins to develop his own individual art, his own imaginative powers, to become a creative artist and to leave the stage of a mere learner and imitator. Up to this point his accomplishments are not yet truly his own. The greater part are both socially determined and socially transmissible, for even his first 'images de traduction' will be derived from 'objective Art' and will be taken bodily from it, just as our—the laymen's—'pictorial general ideas' are far more extensively inspired by pictures than by reality. The foundations of his personal and individual powers are laid by the development of his manual dexterity and by the first imaginative elaboration of the original stock of his imagery. On the basis of these accomplishments, presenting the first fusion of the vision and the technique demanded by his medium, his creative processes are built up. The imaginative complication and enrichment of his conceptions is accompanied by an imaginative refinement and development of their technical formulation, and the farther his artistic imagination breaks away from the traditional stock of his art and becomes more and more his inner personal creation, the deeper and the more sweeping the changes which the simultaneously growing power of his technical imagination introduces into his handling of the medium. Thus new technical processes, new tools and methods, new ways of achieving effects and new solutions of material difficulties are discovered and minister in their turn to the wealth of his artistic imagination.

At this point we run up against perhaps the most formidable and fundamental problem of Æsthetics, that of the artistic imagination. In spite of much writing on the subject, we can hardly be said to have advanced beyond the fringe of the unknown. The chief obstacles to progress seem to me to have been a long-standing confusion of imagery with imagination and the attempt to deal with imagination on far too narrowly intellectualistic a conception of novelty and originality as a characteristic feature of imagination. Imagination is clearly different from and in contrast

N

to normal consciousness, but at the same time overlapping it to a large extent. The imaginative experience such as the artist in particular lives in, is more nearly the imaginative counterpart of actual experience than imaginings wholly outside the range of normal experience—which is true rather of people generally called 'unimaginative'. The novelty and originality of the artistic imagination lies far less in its eccentricity to normal life than in its being the reflection of an intensely and intimately individual experience, transferred to the sphere of imagination, thereby removed from its personal reference and rendered accessible to and effective for the sympathy, understanding and appreciation of others. This curiously dualistic, yet unified psychosis I have attempted to render intelligible as 'distancing'.[1] And the medium, its treatment, its very limitations and the fusion with the artist's vision in Technique, is one of the chief factors of artistic creation, forcing the distancing process upon the artist while at the same time it facilitates the maintenance of distance.

IV. Concerning the relation of mind and medium in *æsthetic appreciation* little need be said. If the principle be accepted that, ideally, appreciation is a re-creation of the work in the mind of the recipient, it follows that the relation in his mind should not differ widely from that in the mind of the artist. The qualification implied in the term '*re*-creation' must not be lost sight of. For I confess that I disagree with the pleasant theory that 'all men are artists'. If we agree upon calling 'artists' those capable of creating Art, the best that we can say for the non-artist is that he is capable of following in appreciation the creative process of the artist, and his capacity even in this respect is notoriously limited.

Again, if, as I believe, the attitude to medium and its technique forms an integral part in the creation of a work, it may be contended that perfect appreciation should also be conscious and

---

[1] Edward Bullough, 'Psychical Distance as a Factor in Art and an æsthetic Principle'. *British Journal of Psychology*, V, 87 ff. [Bullough is clearly using *psychosis* above in its psychological, not its pathological, sense, as 'an activity or movement of the psychic organism'. Ed.]

appreciative of this function. I cannot therefore quite follow Mr. Watt in his statement about 'the great and spontaneous joy that the greatest art gives even to the inexperienced provided they are "pure in heart".' Every appreciation of whatever kind requires a certain experience and education in the matter to be appreciated. I do not, of course, mean a reasoned judgment about it. But I am a little suspicious about the purity in heart. It savours to me of Ruskin and Tolstoy and suggests an uncritical admission into the effect of a work, as æsthetic enjoyment, of all kinds of pleasant impressions which may have nothing whatever to do with it.

I readily admit that you may æsthetically appreciate a work without knowing anything about its technical aspects. But I cannot persuade myself that an appreciation of this side would not materially enhance the appreciation of the whole. To revert to the example of Architecture: an appreciation of the spatial forms is not necessarily dependent upon an appreciation of its structural excellence, as has been and is still contended by Viollet-le-Duc, Ruskin and their 'veristic', moralistic and intellectualistic followers.[1] Structural excellence as such has nothing to do with æsthetic effect. What matters is the *relation* of structure to the space-forms, their subservience to spatial effects and the use made of them to achieve these effects; and I am convinced that an understanding of this relation will considerably increase and deepen the æsthetic appreciation of the whole, not least because it surmounts the dualism of these two sets of factors. But I equally admit the danger of technical knowledge for the layman and this is, I believe, what Mr. Watt alludes to when he demands 'purity in heart' of him. The medium and its handling have tremendous attractions for the layman, as all technical procedures have. The desire to *know* 'how it is done' and all the unholy curiosity stirred by the relative ease of satisfying this desire by a purely intellectual knowledge about it are destructive of all æsthetic appreciation, unless they can be kept subordinate to the attitude of contempla-

---

[1] This point has been admirably dealt with under the name of 'intellectual and moral fallacies' by Mr. Geoffrey Scott in his *Architecture of Humanism*.

tion. The layman has generally neither the respect which the artist naturally feels towards his art, nor his consciousness of the true function of technique, nor his imaginative and emotional control. And it is, after all, so much easier to understand than to appreciate that it is little wonder if in the layman's mind technical knowledge takes precedence over æsthetic appreciation and thereby breaks up the unity of the æsthetic state. But this failure is no argument against the assertion that real appreciation of technique should enter into the total effect of the work with all the enhancement it carries with it, just as it entered into the creative act of the artist.

V. In conclusion I offer a few detached observations on the relation of mind and medium from the point of view of Genetic Æsthetics.

Genetic Æsthetics is the necessary complement to any psychological formulation of æsthetic facts. Psychological Æsthetics can give us an account only of what *we*, at the present time and with our largely local experience, mean by 'Art', æsthetic appreciation and artistic creation, since only our own experiences are directly and to some extent introspectively accessible to us. What the Renaissance, the Middle Ages, the Greeks, Egyptians, Chinese, or the primitive peoples meant when they spoke (many never spoke) of Art is ascertainable only indirectly, on their own critical and theoretic statements.[1] Their works are no unambiguous testimony, doubly obscured as their evidence is by the confusing interpretations on our own analogies through which we have been accustomed to see them. That 'Art' has not, in its history, retained the same significance is beyond doubt. How far was the art-experience of the Greeks, Egyptians or Chinese the same as ours? How has art-experience in general come to be what it is? That is the problem of Genetic Æsthetics. No principle of Æsthetics can, I believe, be regarded as valid, which is not itself capable of evolution and thereby avoids the fallacy of applying to past periods of Art

[1] This constitutes the chief interest and value of past literary and art criticism.

and human society terms which can have meaning only in reference to our present conceptions.

A. As regards Art in the objective sense, it seems to me that the importance and prominence of the material and of the technical tradition have noticeably decreased.

The material itself clearly plays a very considerable part in the estimation placed upon art-objects (if they can always be so called) in primitive 'Art' and much later, even latest, periods of Art-history. The value attaches apparently either to the intrinsic preciousness of the material—something of the kind survives in some of the crafts such as gem-cutting and work in precious metals—or to its magical efficiency, or to the mere difficulty of working it. None of these criteria are in our sense æsthetic, but entered, it seems, largely into the appreciation of former 'Art'. The extreme hardness of Egyptian porphyry probably added much to the value of works executed in it and the reference to it by Vasari[1] suggests that the difficulties of working it even in his day contributed to the estimation of this medium. White jade was reserved in ancient China for the exclusive use of the emperor, on account partly of its rarity, partly of its magical associations, and came to be regarded as the most precious kind of this highly prized material. The chryselephantine statuary of the Greeks must have enjoyed the reputation it had for similar reasons, for we cannot, I think, avoid the suspicion that artistically it must have been an error of judgment.

Technical tradition was notoriously rigid at certain periods to an extent which we would consider inimical to the production of anything that we should call Art. The reasons are very multi-farious and cannot be dealt with here. Stereotyped patterns—stereotyped even so far as to be transferred to media intrinsically unsuitable to them—stereotyped arrangements of colours, of formulas, phrases, cadences, etc., are too well known to be more than mentioned. Ecclesiastical and any kind of hieratic influence

[1] *Vasari on Technique* (ed. with introduction and notes by G. Baldwin Brown.) Dent, 1907, pp. 26 ff.

has always been responsible for such an unbending maintenance of technical tradition, originally no doubt from magical motives. Wherever present, such motives inspired the worker with a quasi-religious awe and helped to prevent the mergence of the medium in his own conceptions, provided he were allowed to entertain such at all. Few artistic phenomena are in this respect more illuminating than Russian Ikon-painting with its rigid adherence to traditional attitudes, subjects, apparel, facial expressions, colours and media. The consequences of convention went so far as to develop a most carefully observed division of labour in the painting of Ikons: one painter specialised in gilding, another in painting dresses, another in backgrounds, another in faces, etc.[1] This specialisation carried with it a technical training of the most exclusive kind. Comparable to it, and in addition permeated with magical motives, is the initiation which was customary among the Bushmen for the training of their painters: apparently the preparation of colours was a magical guild-secret like the preparation of poisons in the same tribe.[2] A similar institution has been suggested by the Abbé Breuil in connection with the palaeolithic paintings in the Altamira Caves.[3]

The medieval guilds—including such as the Meistersingers—though more definitely economic and artistic in essence and object, betray the same preoccupation in the maintenance of technical tradition.

B. In the development of Art from the dynamic point of view, i.e. in the history of creation and appreciation the outstanding fact is the differentiation, first, of the craftsman from the public, and later the differentiation of the artist from the craftsman.

The differentiation of the craftsman from the public is in itself a very complex process which, however, even in primitive societies

---

[1] В. Н. Успенскій: Очерки по исторіи иконописанія. СПЪ. The painters who dealt exclusively with dresses, had the delightful technical name of 'Доличные' (up-to-the-facers), p. 15.

[2] G. W. Stow, *The native races of South Africa*, 1905, p. 76.

[3] Cartailhac et Breuil, *La Caverne d'Altamira*, Monaco, 1906, p. 135.

appears to have at least begun, curiously enough, it seems, especially in connection with music. I mention it as a peculiarly important development for the question before us, inasmuch as it marks the transition from manual dexterity as a *personal* qualification to dexterity as a *professional* qualification of the craftsman. The change is the outward reflection of a psychological shifting to a point of view which is a pre-requisite to an æsthetic attitude. Once the distinction of the craftsman is secured, several other social distinctions develop of which the above-mentioned guild-formations with their consequences for technical tradition and teaching are only one.

The differentiation between the craftsman and the artist is one of the characteristic features of Art since the Renaissance. Indeed, the Greeks appear just to have reached this same point in the development of their social and æsthetic culture, when its course was interrupted by political collapse. The stage was reached again in the fifteenth century. It is, of course, true that Art has never recruited its devotees wholly from the artisan class. Both poets and to a lesser extent musicians were drawn chiefly from other sources, and it is one of the distinguishing traits of Chinese pictorial art that most of its representatives were men of letters rather than craftsmen, a fact which is reflected in the close connection between painting and calligraphy both in China and Japan with far reaching results for the technique and æsthetics of Chinese and Japanese painting.[1]

The shifting of the social status of the executant from craftsman to artist is again merely the outward symptom of a much deeper and more fundamental alteration in the relation to Art of the Middle Ages and modern times respectively. The decay of the apprenticeship-system, the rise of a new Art-education, signalised by the foundation of academies, the removal of Art from its fixed social and economic functions in medieval society to the exercise of a new, economically indetermined and ideally wholly un-

---

[1] R. Petrucci, *Le Kie Tseu Yuan Houa Tchouan*, T'oung-pao, XIII, p. 82 note; also Sei-Ichi Taki, *Three Essays on Oriental Painting*, 1910, p. 25 ff.

fettered vocation are collateral phenomena of this profound change. Psychologically and æsthetically, the nucleus of the new situation is a new conception of Art which since the Renaissance has become the basis for our modern attitude to it. Nothing could be stranger to this modern idea than the position of the medieval craftsman working to specifications of such minuteness as some of the contracts for pictures reveal, as for instance that for the Coronation of the Virgin by Enguerrand Charonton.[1] Nor could any contrast be more striking than that of a comparison between for example the *Schedula diversarum artium* of the Monk Theophilus (probably eleventh century) and the first manifesto of the modern conception: the *Della Pittura* of Leon Battista Alberti, of 1436; especially when you compare the Prologue of Theophilus with the famous opening of Alberti's third book.[2] As an illuminating illustration of this new conception relevant to the present discussion, I quote Alberti's condemnation of the use of gold in paintings, from the end of the second book of his treatise:

> Truovasi chi adopera molto in sue storie oro, che stima porga maësta; non lo lodo. Et benchè dipigniesse quella Didone di Vergilio, ad cui era la pharetra d'oro, i capelli aurei nodati in oro, et la vesta purpurea cinta pur d'oro, i freni al cavallo et ogni cosa d'oro; non però ivi vorrei, punto adoperassi oro però che nei colori imitando i razzi del oro, stà più admiratione et lode al artefice.[3]

The importance of the passage lies, I submit, in the fact that it records the definite loss of the intrinsic value of the medium and the renunciation of the effects of mere material preciousness in the interest of a purely æsthetic homogeneity of style.

[1] See Thomas Okey, *History of Avignon* (Medieval Town Series), pp. 375–9.

[2] A concise and useful summary on several of these points will be found in the Introductory Essay of G. Baldwin Brown's edition of *Vasari on Technique*, Dent, 1907. See also the French edition of *Schedula div. art.* by Ch. de l'Escalopier with an introduction by J. M. Guichard, Paris, 1843.

[3] P. 139 of the *Della Pittura* in the edition by H. Janitschek (*Quellenschr. für Kunstgeschichte*), 1877.

By the end of the fifteenth century the Art of the Italian Renaissance had triumphed over the difficulties of its media and it is significant that one of its greatest representatives, Leonardo, allowed himself to be carried away by his enthusiasm for the rendering of light and of shadows so far as to remark:

> Sola la pittura si rende (cosa maravigliosa) ai contemplatori di quella per far parere rilevato e spiccato dai muri quel che non lo è, ed *i colori sol fanno onore ai maestri che li fanno, perchè in loro non si causa altra maraviglia che bellezza, la quale bellezza non è virtu del pittore, ma di quello che li ha generati.* . . .[1]

Since then the commercial production of media has still further contributed to the loss of their practical importance. The modern painter no longer grinds his own colours and spends years in experiments with different pigments and varnishes. The present-day sculptor orders the block of marble he wants; he no longer selects and even quarries it himself as Michelangelo did. As likely as not he will leave the transfer of his model to marble or bronze to a firm of contractors.

It is true that there are two media which cannot be standardised, commercialised, contracted for. They have consequently never lost and never will lose the peculiar position which the uniqueness of a medium secures for it in artistic creation and appreciation. They are the human voice, and the human body as the vehicle of its soul. Singing and acting are the two arts which achieved their distinctive æsthetic value, the former almost from the beginnings, the latter relatively very early in the history of Art.

That the growth of mechanical aids constitutes a great danger to Art which, I venture to think, has not failed to make itself felt in our times, will probably be admitted. All æsthetic psychoses are very complex states poised in a highly unstable equilibrium. This applies to the individual attitude as much as to that of whole

---

[1] Quoted from the 'Trattato della Pittura' in Lionello Venturi, *La Critica e l'Arte di Leonardo da Vinci*, Zanichelli, no date, but 1919.

periods, and æsthetically the functions of the medium, though subordinate to the mind of the artist, cannot be decreased beyond a certain point without the disturbance of this balance, without emasculating imagination, allowing dilettantism to usurp the place of art, and ultimately without the loss of the most precious æsthetic quality of a work: its intrinsic style.